STEP BY STEP IN
WOODWORKING

STEP BY STEP IN
WOODWORKING

A W P Kettless

HAMLYN

London · New York · Sydney · Toronto

First published 1972

© Copyright The Hamlyn Publishing Group Limited, 1972
Published by The Hamlyn Publishing Group Limited
London · New York · Sydney · Toronto
Hamlyn House, Feltham, Middlesex, England
Printed in Great Britain by Cox and Wyman, Fakenham,
Norfolk

ISBN 600 33904 1

Contents

Introduction

For the economical production of domestic furniture, well-equipped modern workshops are necessary, together with the staff to operate the machinery, to assemble the components and to finish the various pieces to the required standard.

The home worker, making furniture or smaller articles of use or decoration by hand, not only saves himself a considerable amount of money but practises a craft which provides recreation, mental stimulation and a good deal of satisfaction.

However, the satisfaction is greater and the finished job better if, instead of embarking hopefully on a project which is slightly beyond his capacity, the amateur has been shown the skills and techniques necessary in advance, and has perhaps even practised them on simpler (but still useful) jobs. There is a world of difference between an article made by a man who is systematically learning basic woodworking skills and that made by an amateur 'jumping in at the deep end'.

I have planned this book to encourage and help the beginner to develop his skills in an interesting and progressive manner. I feel sure that the home woodworker, while learning his craft, does not want to practise making joints and so on using odd pieces of wood which are then discarded. Right from the start he wants to make things, and to make them properly. Yet, as with all skills, practice makes perfect and there is no short cut. Therefore, in this book, the reader is guided through the basic woodwork techniques whilst at the same time he is shown how to make practice pieces of some tangible value, such as wall plaques and various abstract forms. This approach is seen quite clearly in the chapter 'Practice and Simple Jobs'.

The woodworking projects which make up the main part of the book are graded as far as possible in order of difficulty and the man who worked through them all in order could claim at the end to have reached a certain level of proficiency. However, it is not necessary, of course, to make them all: the descriptions and detailed drawings for each object are quite self-contained and intelligible to the learner.

The projects were all designed and made by me, and my finished work is shown in the photographs. It is hoped that the procedure notes, cutting lists and information on materials will help all those interested in this absorbing subject to become more proficient in craftsmanship and appreciative of design. It is appreciated that good design is subjective, and therefore I have shown, where possible, how variations to the basic design can be made to suit individual tastes without the project becoming more difficult. Indeed, in many cases the variations show how the job can be made easier if the amateur feels that some aspect of the work is beyond his present skills.

The cottage furniture illustrated—dining table, chairs, settee and square coffee table—was designed to be made with the minimum amount of material and to a limited budget. (It should be noted that all the project designs in this book are the author's copyright.)

A basic kit of tools is suggested below; the reader will naturally build up his kit gradually, remembering that it is a good investment to buy only the best brands. To enable the reader to purchase wisely and to equip himself with the essential requirements, the tools in each section of the basic kit have been arranged as near as possible in order of importance to the beginner.

All the sizes given in the cutting lists for the various projects are, unless otherwise stated, finished sizes. It is common practice to make all dimensions of length oversize, and an allowance of approximately 10mm. has been made in these lists. Dimensions have been given in millimetres throughout, as the metric system is coming into general use, but the sizes of the various projects are chosen for easy conversion into inches. It is expected that during the metrication transition period wood will be sold in both inches and millimetres, and for those who prefer to work in inches, or who can better visualise an article described in inches, a metric conversion table is also given below.

BASIC KIT OF TOOLS
Saws
Cross-cut, length 660mm., 8–9 points
Tenon, length 305mm., 14 points
Coping and fret saw
Dovetail, length 200mm., 19–22 points

Planes
Smoothing (metal), 50mm. cutter
Jack (metal), 60mm. cutter
Rebate (rabbet) and Fillister (metal)
Block plane
Spokeshave (flat)
Shoulder plane
Wood file, 200mm.
Wood rasp, 200mm.
Stanley 'Surform' files

Marking and Testing Tools
Folding rule, 1 metre (wood)
Try square, 150mm.

Steel rule (can also be used as a straight edge)
Marking knife
Marking gauge
Combination square

Chisels
Firmer, 12mm., 18mm. and 25mm.
Sash mortise, 6mm.
Bevelled edge firmer, 6mm., 25mm.
Gouge, 12mm. No. 6 carving

Tools for Boring
Bradawl
Brace, 200mm. sweep.
Twist bits, 6mm., 9mm., 12mm. and 25mm.
Wheelbrace
Drills, twist, 2mm. to 6mm.
Countersink, rosehead, 12mm.

Sharpening Accessories
Oilstone, fine, 200mm. × 50mm. × 25mm. in box
Oilcan
Oilstone, medium, 200mm. × 50mm. × 25mm. in box
Oilstone slip, 100mm.
1 piece of leather, 200mm. × 50mm. (for strop)

Miscellaneous
Mallet
Hammer, Warrington, 8oz. (225 grammes)
Pincers, 200mm.
Screwdriver, cabinet pattern, 200mm.
Screwdriver, ratchet, 150mm.
Nail punch, medium
'G' cramps, two, 150mm.
Sash cramps, two, 750mm.

CONVERSION TABLE

Inches to millimetres (to nearest workable number)

in.	mm.	in.	mm.	in.	mm.	in.	mm.	in.	mm.	in.	mm.	in.	mm.	in.	mm.
$\frac{1}{16}$	1·5	2	50	11	275	20	505	29	735	38	965	47	1,190	56	1,420
$\frac{1}{8}$	3	3	75	12	305	21	530	30	760	39	990	48	1,220	57	1,445
$\frac{1}{4}$	6	4	100	13	330	22	555	31	785	40	1,015	49	1,245	58	1,470
$\frac{3}{8}$	9	5	125	14	355	23	580	32	810	41	1,040	50	1,270	59	1,495
$\frac{1}{2}$	12·5	6	150	15	380	24	610	33	835	42	1,065	51	1,295	60	1,520
$\frac{5}{8}$	16	7	175	16	405	25	635	34	860	43	1,090	52	1,320	72	1,830
$\frac{3}{4}$	19	8	200	17	430	26	660	35	885	44	1,115	53	1,345	84	2,135
$\frac{7}{8}$	22	9	225	18	455	27	685	36	915	45	1,140	54	1,370	96	2,440
1	25	10	250	19	480	28	710	37	940	46	1,165	55	1,395	108	2,745

Timber and Manufactured Boards

Wood is one of the world's most versatile materials. It can be obtained in a wide variety of sizes, colours and textures. It can be worked with edge tools—saws, planes and chisels, etc.—and it is used extensively in the building and furniture industries. Even the waste is utilized in the production of hardboard, chipboard and other man-made materials.

Trees have a complex cellular structure and are divided into two main categories: (a) hardwood or broad-leaved trees, (b) softwood or needle-leaved trees. The latter are usually cone bearing and are often referred to as conifers.

Fig. 1A shows a section through a tree. The main parts are:

(a) growth rings—these consist of springwood (the light inner part of the ring) and summerwood (the denser portion of the ring);

(b) sapwood—this is the outer portion of the tree, usually light in colour, softer and of inferior quality than the heartwood;

(c) rays—these act as ducts to store and convey food to all parts of the tree;

(d) heartwood—this is the dark inner portion of the tree, producing the most durable timber for commercial purposes;

(e) bark—this surrounds the tree and forms a protective covering especially for new growth.

Conversion After the tree is felled it is necessary to 'break down' the log—that is to saw it into smaller sections—as soon as possible. This process is called conversion. Fig. 1B and C illustrate the two main forms of conversion. The most economical is the through and through, flat or slash sawn method. The quarter sawn method produces timber which is more stable, and in some instances—particularly oak—better figured. Owing to the extra work involved in converting a quarter sawn log, timber converted this way is much dearer.

Before freshly cut or green timber can be used for constructional purposes it must be carefully seasoned to meet the requirements of the consumer. Most timber yards have a variety of logs stacked for seasoning. The stacking is very carefully arranged, with piling sticks placed at short intervals between every plank to allow the air to circulate freely around the planks or boards. This method is known as natural or air seasoning, and it is a slow process, taking approximately one year for every inch of thickness, and it leaves the wood with a moisture content of about 18 per cent.

Kiln seasoning is an artificial and rapid method of seasoning, by which means timber can be conditioned to suit any particular requirements.

Defects to be avoided The information given below will help you to select your timber requirements with confidence.

Knots Although generally to be avoided, for some jobs knots could be decorative, for example knotty pine panelling. Make sure the knots are sound and not loose, and are not likely to fall out.

Twisting This is the spiral warping of a board or plank in a longitudinal direction. See Fig. 1D.

Cupping This is warping across the width of the board, and does not occur in quarter sawn timber. See Fig. 1E

End splits End splits are the separation or rupture of the wood tissue, extending to both sides of the board. See Fig. 1F.

Bowing The warping or sagging from end to end of a board or plank is called bowing. It is often caused by careless stacking. See Fig. 1G.

Sapwood The outer portion of a tree, usually of

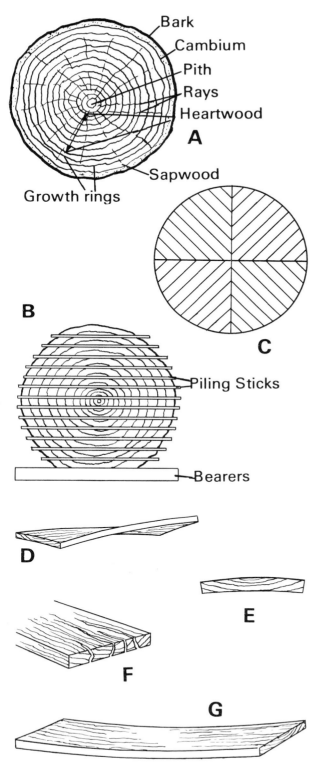

Bark
Cambium
Pith
Rays
Heartwood

A

Sapwood

Growth rings

B

C

Piling Sticks

Bearers

D

E

F

G

inferior quality than heartwood. It is liable to be attacked by woodworm.

Get to know your local timber merchants. Some will stock only softwoods, while others will cater mainly for hardwood. Very often small pieces of hardwood lying around the yard are suitable for carving and can be purchased for a modest sum. Your local do-it-yourself shop may be able to supply your softwood needs. Before visiting your timber merchant, make sure you know exactly what you want, and have a cutting list prepared for him.

Wood that is imported into Britain is usually in the sawn state, as cut or converted by the mill which prepared it for export. This material can be purchased in the sawn sizes. Most softwood merchants keep a good stock of standard sizes of prepared timber and mouldings. If you require your material planed all round, simply specify P.A.R. This means that the sawn material has been planed all round and the planing will have made it approximately 3mm. ($\frac{1}{8}$in.) smaller in width and thickness. You must remember this when ordering. Not all hardwood merchants are equipped with planing machines, so you may have to prepare your own timber to the finished sizes, or arrange for a local joiner's shop to do this for you.

MANUFACTURED BOARDS

Plywood One of the best known boards, plywood consists of an odd number of veneers in sheet form, laid and glued together so that the grain of each piece is at right angles to that of the next (see Fig. 2A.) This arrangement of veneers or plies gives plywood its special qualities, such as stability (no shrinkage or warping as in solid timber), strength and flexibility. A good range of sizes are available from $1\frac{1}{2}$mm. ($\frac{1}{16}$in.) thick.
Multi-ply This is the term used for plywood of five or more plies.
Laminboard Very stable, laminboard is suitable for high-class furniture. It is one of the more expensive boards. The core is made up of slats of veneer or thin wood not exceeding 7mm. ($\frac{1}{4}$in.) in thickness, and is faced on both sides with one or more veneers (see Fig. 2B).

Fig. 1. Timber and some defects. A : section through tree, B : through and through or slash sawn timber, C : method of quarter sawing, D : twisting, E : cupping, F : end-splits, G : bowing

9

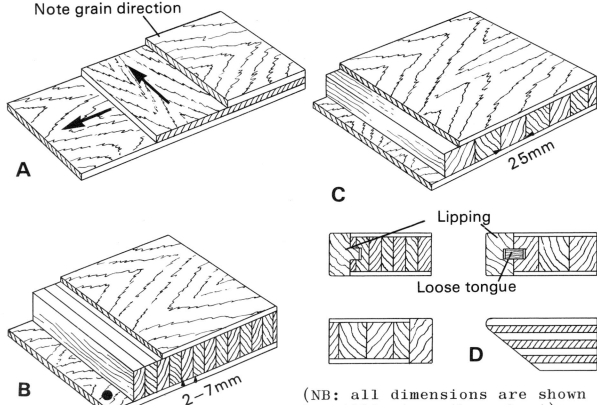

Note grain direction

A

B

2–7mm

C

25mm

Lipping

Loose tongue

D

(NB: all dimensions are shown
in millimetres throughout)

*Fig. 2. Manufactured boards. A : plywood, B : lamin-
board, D : a variety of edge treatments*

Blockboard Similar to laminboard, blockboard
has a core made up of blocks not exceeding
25mm. (1in.) wide. It is very good for table tops,
doors, etc., but is not so stable as laminboard.
See Fig. 2C.

Hardboard This consists of wood fibre formed
into a cohesive slab, which is subjected to great
pressure at a very high temperature, making a
tough and durable board. A wide variety of hardboards is available, including perforated hardboard or pegboard, hardboard surfaced with
melamine, plastic-faced, veneered, moulded or
embossed, painted, etc. This versatile material is
now used in large quantities in industry and by
home craftsmen. It is used for flushing doors,
panelling, floor covering, trays, table tops, etc. It
is easily worked with ordinary hand tools. Use a
fine-toothed saw when cutting to size. Hardboard is obtainable in a wide range of large
sheets in thicknesses varying from $2\frac{1}{2}$ to 18mm.
($\frac{3}{32}$ to $\frac{3}{4}$in.)

Wood Chipboard A constructional board consisting of softwood chips, finely milled to a uni-

form size and bonded with ureaformaldehyde
synthetic resin, chipboard is used for doors,
shelving, cupboards, flooring, etc. It can be purchased veneered on both sides. Thickness
generally ranges from 12 to 18mm. ($\frac{1}{2}$ to $\frac{3}{4}$in.).

Edge Treatments Lipping is used to finish the
edges of multi-ply, laminboard, blockboard, etc.
Fig. 2D shows a variety of edge treatments suitable for table tops and doors.

TIMBERS AND THEIR USES

A variety of timbers have been used in the making of the various projects in this book, and a few
of these timbers, with notes on their workability
and uses, are discussed below.

Softwood

(a) Scots pine. Also known as 'deal', Scots pine
generally works easily and cleanly. This wood

takes nails well, and gives good results with paint, varnish and polish. It is used in all kinds of construction work. Top grades are used in joinery and furniture making.

(b) Douglas fir (Columbian pine). Top-grade Douglas fir works well, provided tools are kept sharp. The timber takes screws and nails satisfactorily. Its uses are in carpentry, joinery, pine furniture.

(c) Cedar. Easily worked with sharp tools, cedar provides a good finish. It is used in joinery, cabinet making, garden furniture.

(d) Parana pine. This wood can be obtained in good lengths and widths. It works well but should be used before it has a chance to warp. If storing, store carefully in stick and check occasionally. Parana pine is used in joinery and cabinet making.

Hardwoods

(a) Utile. This wood generally works well, and has good gluing and screwing properties. In colour it is similar to mahogany, and is used in joinery and furniture making, etc.

(b) Chestnut. Mild and easy to work, chestnut takes glue well, and polishes satisfactorily. It is used in furniture, particularly interior work such as drawer sides and framing, etc.

(c) Oak. With clean straight-grained oak timber a good finish can easily be obtained with sharp tools. Oak is used in the ship-building, building and furniture industries, and is well known for its strength and durability.

(d) Guarea. In colour similar to pale mahogany, guarea generally works fairly easily. It is used in furniture and high-class joinery.

(e) Lime. This wood works cleanly and easily and is very good for turning and carving.

(f) Teak. Fairly easy to work providing that tools are sharpened frequently, teak is used in ship-building, furniture, joinery, garden furniture. It is also suitable for carving and turnery.

Woodworking Tools

This chapter briefly introduces the principal tools used in woodworking, with information on their use and maintenance. The home craftsman will also find it useful to have an electric power tool with a range of attachments and accessories.

SAWS

Saws used by the woodworker fall into two categories: (a) for ripping, that is cutting along the grain, and (b) for cross-cutting, that is sawing across the grain.

Ripsaw Recommended size: length 660mm. (26in.), 4 points to the inch. It is economical to use a power tool with a circular saw where a large quantity of timber has to be ripped to size. Fig. 3A shows the outline of the teeth, with an end view of the saw blade showing 'set'.

Cross-cut or Hand saw This is a very popular and useful saw (Fig. 3B). Recommended size: length 660mm. (26in.), 8 points to the inch. The teeth on the cross-cut saw are sharpened at an angle which produces needle-like points, enabling the

Fig. 3. Saws. A : ripsaw teeth, B : crosscut saw, C : crosscut saw teeth, D : tenon saw, E : fret saw, F : pad-saw, G : coping saw

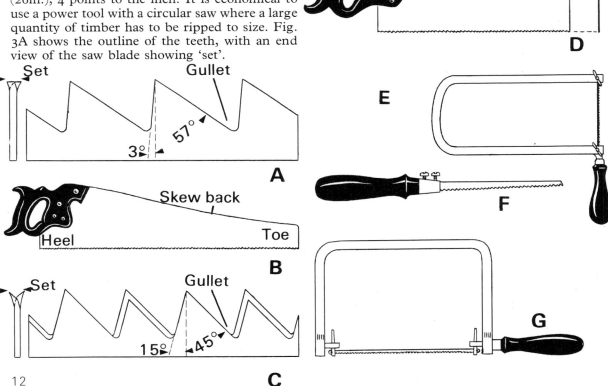

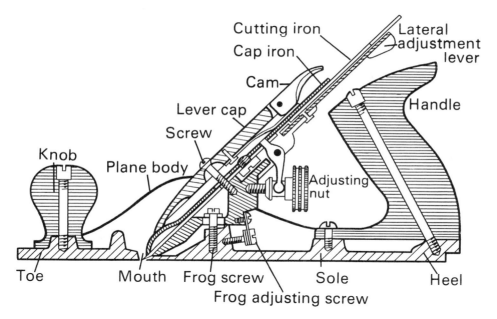

Cutting iron • Lateral adjustment lever
Cap iron
Cam
Lever cap • Handle
Screw
Knob
Plane body • Adjusting nut
Toe • Mouth • Frog screw • Sole • Heel
Frog adjusting screw

Fig. 4. Sectional view of metal plane

saw to cut cleanly across the grain. These saws can also be used for cutting thin material along the grain. Fig. 3C shows the outline of the teeth of a cross-cut saw.

Panel saw Recommended size: length 555mm. (22in.), 11 points to the inch. Smaller than the handsaw, it is used for fine work, such as cross-cutting thin panels, plywood and laminboard, etc.

Tenon saw This saw (Fig. 3D) is most useful for general purposes as well as for cutting tenons and dovetails, etc. It is sometimes called a back saw, and has a back of steel or brass. Recommended size: length 305mm. (12in.), 14 points to the inch.

Coping saw Blade length: 150mm. (6in.). This saw (Fig. 3G) is used for cutting fine curves, removing waste in dovetailing and the scribing of mouldings.

Fret saw A fret saw (Fig. 3E) is particularly useful for cutting shapes in plywood.

Keyhole or pad saw Blade length: 305mm. (12in.). This saw (Fig. 3F) is used for small work particularly where there is limited space to operate or where a larger saw would be an obstruction.

Dovetail saw A dovetail saw is used mainly for cutting dovetails and other fine work.

PLANES

Planes are important tools used by the woodworker to work and shape wood to given sizes, and to prepare surfaces for different finishes.

Wood jack plane Made of selected beech, a wood jack plane is an indispensible tool for the crafts-

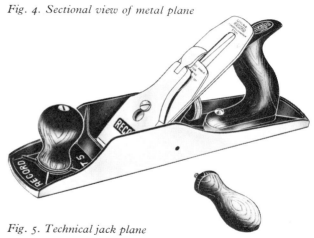

Fig. 5. Technical jack plane

Fig. 6. Smoothing plane

Fig. 7. Block plane

Fig. 8. Rebate (rabbet) plane

Fig. 9. Typical examples of rebating

 Rebate

 Rebates to take plywood

 Picture frame moulding

Fig. 10. Router

Fig. 11. Use of router

Stopped housing

Depth of housing should equal approx. $\frac{1}{3}$ thickness of material

Fig. 12. Shoulder plane

Shoulder of tenon

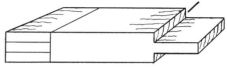

Fig. 13. Use of shoulder plane
Fig. 14. Plough plane

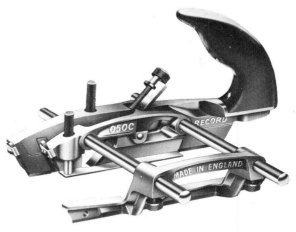

Fig. 15. Use of plough plane

Plough groove

 Panel

Part of framing

Tray bottom

man. It needs expert attention to maintain in good condition. A useful size is 405mm. (16in.) long with 57mm. ($2\frac{1}{4}$in.) cutter.

Metal jack plane Recommended size: 380mm. (15in.) long, 60mm. ($2\frac{3}{8}$in.) cutter. The modern metal planes are reliable, easily adjusted, and, if used in the normal way, will remain flat and true for many years. Fig. 4 shows the sectional elevation of a metal plane. Fig. 5 shows a technical jack plane, with side handle for use on the shooting board.

Smoothing plane Recommended size: 225mm. (9in.) long with 50mm. (2in.) cutter. A smoothing plane is necessary for cleaning up (preparing surfaces for polish or paint, etc.) and general bench work (see Fig. 6).

Block plane Smaller than the smoothing plane, a block plane can be held comfortably in one hand. It has a low-angled iron, and is particularly useful for small work and the cleaning up of end grain (see Fig. 7).

Rebate (rabbet) and fillister plane A very useful and versatile plane, a rebate plane is shown in Fig. 8, and typical examples of its work in Fig. 9.

Router Essential when finishing housings or grooves to depth, is a router (see Fig. 10). Its work is shown in Fig. 11.

Shoulder plane A shoulder plane is a low-pitched plane for trimming shoulders and cleaning up rebates, and is generally useful for accurate work. The Record No. 311 plane can be used as either a shoulder or a bullnose plane (see Fig. 12). An example of its use is shown in Fig. 13.

Plough plane A plough plane is for making grooves, particularly for panels. Fig. 14 shows a plough plane and Fig. 15 its uses.

Spokeshave A spokeshave (Fig. 16) is a type of plane for shaping and finishing work (Fig. 17) after using the bow or coping saw. It is available with a flat or round bottom.

Rasps and Files Rasps and files (see Fig. 18) are essential shaping tools but they are used only when edge tools cannot be used efficiently. They are used for the shaping of hand holes for trays, shaped dishes, carving etc.

MARKING OUT AND TESTING TOOLS
Steel rule A steel rule is essential for measuring and testing (Fig. 19A).

Wood rule A 2ft. (610mm.) four-fold boxwood rule is useful for general purposes. A metre (39·4in.) four-fold wood rule is also obtainable.

Winding strips Essential for testing material for

Fig. 16. *Spokeshave*

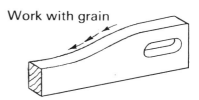

Work with grain

Fig. 17. *Use of spokeshave*

Fig. 18. *Stanley Surform rasps and files*

wind, a useful size of winding strip (Fig. 19B) is 355mm. (14in.). It is usually made by the craftsman.

Try square A try square (Fig. 19E) is for testing the squareness of material and for marking out.

Combination square A popular size for a combination square is 150mm. (6in.). It can be used as a depth gauge, mitre square (Fig. 19D) and for testing rebates (Fig. 19C), etc.

Marking gauge For marking lines down the length and ends of material (Fig. 19F).

Mortise gauge A mortise gauge (Fig. 19G) is essential for marking out mortise and tenon joints and have two spurs, adjustable to seat the width of the mortise chisel.

Marking knife For making clean-cut lines for

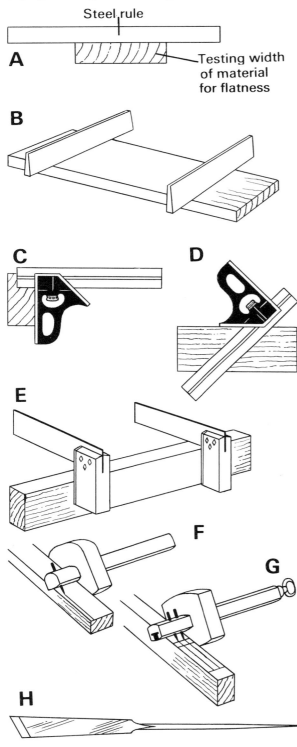

Fig. 19. Marking out and testing tools

Steel rule

A Testing width of material for flatness

B

C

D

E

F

G

H

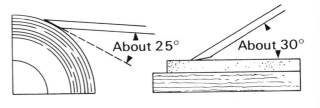

About 25° About 30°

Grinding angle   Sharpening angle

Fig. 20. Grinding and sharpening angles for chisels and planes

shoulders, housing, squaring up ends of material, etc., a marking knife (Fig. 19H) is used.

CHISELS AND GOUGES

Chisels and gouges are used to remove waste in the shaping of wood. The term 'paring' means the removal of wood by means of thin shavings. Chisel sizes are based on the width of blades or length of cutting edge. The grinding and sharpening angles recommended for general use are 25 deg. and 30 deg. respectively. These angles are suitable for planes as well as chisels (see Fig. 20). Fig. 21 shows a selection of these tools.

Types of Chisels

(a) Firmer: A strong robust chisel used for general work (Fig. 21C).
(b) Bevelled edged firmer: Used for general work and for finer work, such as dovetailing (Fig. 21A).
(c) Paring: A paring chisel has a longer blade than the firmer chisel, and is used for fine work; it should never be struck with a mallet. Fig. 21B shows this chisel with the handle removed to show the tang.
(d) Mortise: The blade of a mortise chisel is heavier than that of other chisels. This chisel is designed to withstand leverage and mallet blows. The type shown in Fig. 21E is most used with softwoods and mild-working hardboards.
(e) Registered chisel: Made with an extra ferrule to resist heavy blows, this chisel (Fig. 21D) is useful for all types of carpentry work.

Types of Gouges

(a) Scribing: A scribing gouge (Fig. 21F) is for scribing mouldings and shaping.
(b) Firmer: For hollowing out. A firmer gouge (Fig. 21G) is a good tool for removing waste quickly before work is finished with carving tools.

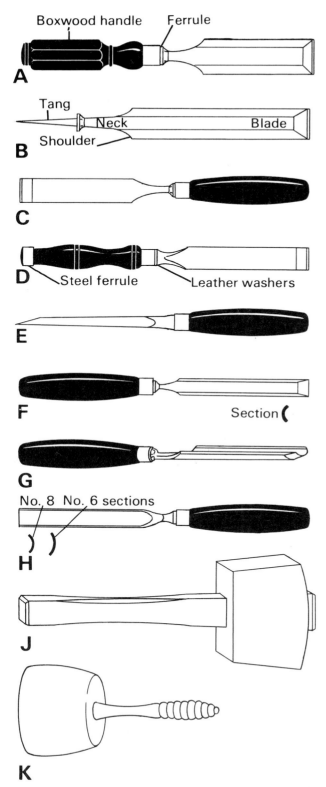

Boxwood handle · **Ferrule**

A

Tang · **Neck** · **Blade**

Shoulder

B

C

D Steel ferrule · Leather washers

E

F Section (

G

No. 8 No. 6 sections

H

J

K

Fig. 21. Chisels, gouges and mallets

(c) Carving: Obtainable in a wide range of sizes and shapes, a carving gouge is shown in Fig. 21H. A set suitable for a large variety of work would be a 16mm. ($\frac{5}{8}$in.) No. 8, a 12·7mm. ($\frac{1}{2}$in.) No. 8 and a 12·7mm. ($\frac{1}{2}$in.) No. 6.

Grinding Edge Tools

Grinding should be done on a wet grindstone, which will not overheat the tool, and thus 'draw the temper' of the steel.

Sharpening Edge Tools

A good oilstone is essential for the efficient sharpening of edge tools. Fig. 22 shows the sharpening of a plane iron on a stone. A fine-grade India (an artificial stone) when used with a light-grade machine oil as a lubricant is very effective, and will produce a very keen edge. The wire edge should be removed on the oilstone. The plane iron or chisel must be kept flat on the stone (see Fig. 23) and finally stropped on a piece of supple leather.

BORING TOOLS

Brace The brace (Fig. 24B) is commonly known as the carpenter's brace or sway. The chuck is designed to hold the various bits used by the woodworker. A screwdriver bit is shown in Fig. 24E. Braces are made in three sweep sizes, 8, 10 and 12in. (200, 250 and 305mm.) and are of plain or ratchet type.

Wheel brace or hand drill A very efficient tool, a wheel brace (Fig. 24K) is designed to hold a range of twist drills and countersinks (see below).

Bradawl A bradawl (Fig. 24F) is for making small holes for screws and nails. It should be kept sharp by filing.

Twist bits A twist bit (Fig. 24G) is used for accurate boring of holes. The dowel bit is shorter than the standard pattern.

Centre bits The boring of holes in thin material requires a centre bit.

Countersinks Countersinks (Fig. 24C) are used for the countersinking of holes to take screw heads.

Twist drill Used in the wheel brace or electric drill, a twist drill (Fig. 24D) is essential for the boring of holes to take screws, nails and small bolts. Various sizes suit the respective sizes of screws.

Flatbit Used for boring holes, a flatbit (Fig. 24A) is very useful for use in an electric drill.

Fig. 22. Sharpening a plane iron   Fig. 23. Removing the wire edge

MISCELLANEOUS TOOLS

Hammer Chiefly used for driving in nails. The Warrington pattern (Fig. 26A) is favoured by joiners and cabinet makers. The claw hammer is popular with carpenters because of the ease with which nails can be withdrawn with its claw.

Mallet Joiner's mallets (Fig. 21J) are used when assembling work and for striking the handles of chisels, gouges, etc. when hand pressure is not sufficient.

Carving mallet The special advantage of a carving mallet (Fig. 21K) is that any part of the head can be used.

Screwdriver Useful sizes and types of screwdriver are 8in. (200mm.) cabinet pattern (Fig. 24H) and 6in. (150mm.) ratchet pattern. Fig. 24J shows a screwdriver used with Pozidriv screws.

Nail punch For sinking nail heads below the surface of the wood, a nail punch (Fig. 26C) is required.

Pincers Pincers are used for withdrawing bent nails, etc. A tower pattern is shown in Fig. 26D.

'G' Cramps For cramping up and holding work securely while shaping, etc., 'G' cramps (Fig. 26B) of sizes 2in. (50mm.) to about 8in. (200mm.) are useful.

Sash cramps Sash cramps (Fig. 26E) are for cramping up doors, frames, carcases, etc. Useful sizes are 24in., 36in., and 48in., (610, 915 and 1,220mm.).

Fig. 25. A useful selection of bits manufactured by William Ridgway and Sons Ltd.

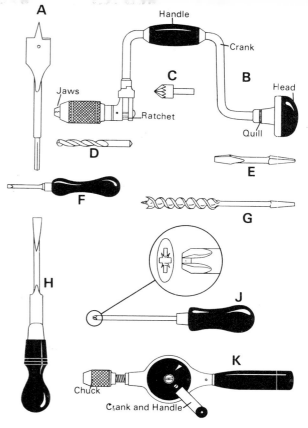

Fig. 24. A selection of boring tools and screwdrivers. A : flatbit, B : brace, C : countersink, D : twist drill, E : screwdriver bit, F : bradawl, G : twist bit, H : cabinet pattern screwdriver, J : Pozidriv screwdriver, K : wheelbase

Fig. 26. A selection of miscellaneous tools. A : Warrington pattern hammer, B : 'G' cramp, C : nail punch, E : sash cramp

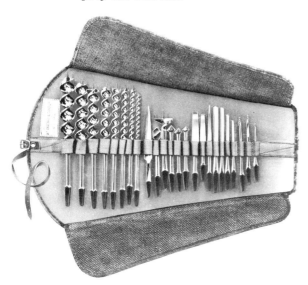

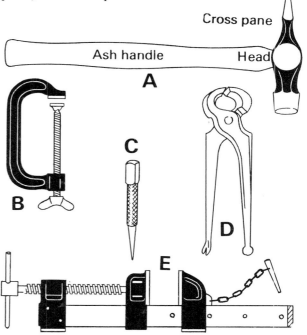

Gluing and Finishing Wood

A large range of glues is manufactured, but those most suitable for the woodworker come into two main categories, animal and synthetic.

ANIMAL GLUES

Scotch glue, which is made from the skins and bones of animals, is the best-known animal glue. This glue is marketed in slab form and in bead form (pearl glue).

Preparation The slab kind should be broken up and left in some water overnight to soak. Pearl glue (small beads of glue) because of its size quickly absorbs water and simplifies preparation. The glue jelly should be heated in a glue pot having a double container to prevent overheating. The glue will be seriously weakened if allowed to burn, and constant checking and attention is necessary. The glue must be used hot and should not be too thick. It should run freely off the brush and not be of a jam-like consistency. Gluing up should be done in a workshop which is warm and free from draughts.

Advantages Scotch glue is simple to use providing precautions are taken not to burn or overheat the glue. It is light in colour and not liable to stain the wood. It does not dull the cutting edges of tools to the same extent as synthetic glues during the cleaning up process. It is very strong and does not become brittle. Scotch glue is excellent for rubbed joints, for gluing up chairs and stools, and veneering, and is generally a cheap versatile glue.

Disadvantages Scotch glue should not be used for external work in damp situations or where there is the possiblility of prolonged heating. Being a hot type of glue, it chills quickly thus limiting the assembly time.

Croid Croid is another form of animal glue, and is obtainable in tins for either hot or cold use.

SYNTHETIC GLUES

Two well-known makes of resin glue are Aerolite and Cascamite. These and similar modern glues have influenced design, construction and production over the whole of the woodworking industry. They are widely used in the manufacture of laminated structures for building, timber engineering, in the moulding and shaping of component parts for furniture and in the making of waterproof plywood for boat building, among other things.

Preparation The glue must be used according to the manufacturer's instructions.

Aerolite Aerolite can be purchased in various grades to suit specific requirements. For home use, Aerolite 306, which consists of a powder and a hardener, is simple to use. The powder is mixed with water to make the resin liquid. This is applied to one part of the joint, and when it makes contact with the hardener or accelerator—which is applied to the other part of the joint—a chemical action is set up, which sets the resin rockhard. The resin liquid can be applied with a clean brush, a piece of wood or a rubber roller. The hardener cap can be applied with a clean brush, which must be free from metal fittings, or with a stick which has a felt pad tied to it.

Cascamite One Shot The resin and the hardener are incorporated in powder form and the glue is ready for use when mixed with water. The glue is simply applied to both parts of the joint with a stick. Care is needed when mixing quantities, as any glue remaining will harden and be wasted.

Advantages Cascamite One Shot is very strong, unaffected by moisture and completely resistant to attack by mould and insects. It rarely stains. A longer period for assembly is available as the setting time can be extended according to type of hardener used.

Disadvantages This glue is expensive to use. Any surplus glue dries rock-hard, and is difficult to remove. It also tends to dull edge tools when cleaning up.

P.V.A. (Polyvinyl Acetate) Glues Based on vinyl resins, P.V.A. glues are the latest development in the range of synthetic adhesives. They are very versatile, and can be used to glue wood, hardboard, tiles, plastics, fabrics, etc.

Preparation No preparation is required as they are applied to the work direct from the container. They are white in colour and non-staining.

Advantages P.V.A. glues have an indefinite storage life if kept away from freezing conditions, though they should be stirred occasionally. They can be applied with a brush or stick.

Disadvantages These glues are not waterproof, nor suitable for high temperatures or humidities.

Contact or Impact Adhesives These glues are of the rubber latex type, and are comparatively simple to use. Adhesion takes place immediately the joint surfaces touch. Ideal for bonding Formica laminates to multiply or laminboard in the making of table tops, dinner wagons and trays, etc.

WOOD FINISHING

Wood with few exceptions needs some kind of surface treatment to protect it, to enable it to be cleaned easily, to enhance the beauty of the grain, and to counteract the effect of changing atmospheric conditions. Before any particular finish can be applied to a job in wood, the surface or surfaces must be carefully prepared. The defects of a surface which has been badly finished always appear much magnified after polishing.

POLISHING

Given below is the procedure necessary for the preparation of the surfaces of any job in hardwood or softwood which is to be given a white French or transparent polish, or other similar finish.

1. Carefully remove all surface glue before planing.

2. Use (according to the size of job) a sharp steel jack or smoothing plane to flush all joints. Occasionally test the work with a straight edge to ensure that all surfaces are flat and true.

3. Clean up flat surfaces with a smoothing plane. Sharpen and set your plane to remove a fine shaving. It is advisable before using it to try it out on a spare piece of wood and adjust the iron as

necessary. When cleaning up a frame take care not to damage the corners.

4. Remove any plane marks and other small blemishes with a cabinet scraper. Note: generally softwoods do not need scraping.

5. Sandpaper. The use of abrasive paper is generally necessary for the final finishing of a surface prior to polishing. It may be glasspaper—commonly called sandpaper—garnet cloth or other material.

To obtain a professional finish sandpaper must be used very carefully. Too often work that should be left with a sharp arris—edge— is rounded by the careless use of sandpaper. For best results the sandpaper should be wrapped round a cork rubber or flat piece of wood, and not held loosely in the hand when going over the work. When using the cork rubber, work in the direction of the grain to minimise scraping the surface. Work through the various grades of sandpaper finishing with a fine grade.

6. Dampen the surface with clean water, allow to dry, and then lightly rub down in the direction of the grain with flour-grade sandpaper. This prevents the initial coat of polish raising the grain.

7. Apply the polish sparingly with a brush (polisher's mop type) or pad, using two or three thin coats rather than one heavy one.

Wax polishing For good results, prepare the work as described above for white or transparent polish, and give the job one coat of white polish. This seals the grain and makes a good sound base for a wax polish. Rub the polished surface down lightly with flour-grade sandpaper, or fine steel wool which has been dipped in wax for lubrication, and then lightly cover the surface with a good wax paste. Polish hard with a soft cloth.

Oil polishing Woods suitable for oil polishing are teak, mahogany, rosewood, walnut, yew and laburnum. For a simple oil finish, gently warm a mixture of 60 per cent linseed oil and 40 per cent pure turps. Apply this sparingly and rub vigorously into the wood. Allow to dry thoroughly before making further applications. Several applications over a period of a few weeks should give lasting results and a good finish.

Finishing kitchen woodware Give salad bowls and wood servers, cheese boards, etc. an occasional wipe over with olive oil.

Care of polishing brushes and rubbers Rubbers should be kept in an airtight tin. Brushes and polishing mops must be washed out with methylated spirits immediately after use.

Polyurethane For a very hard and heatproof finish, polyurethane may be used. This should be applied strictly in accordance with the maker's instructions.

PAINTING

Prepare a surface to take a painted finish as follows:

1. If nails have been used on the job, make sure that all the nail heads are punched in below the surface.

2. Using a sharp and finely set steel jack plane, flush all joints, carefully testing for flatness. In this operation only the minimum amount of wood should be removed.

3. With sandpaper, M2 grade, wrapped firmly round the cork rubber, commence working diagonally across the grain. The light scratches left by the sandpaper form a good key for the paint.

4. Dust all surfaces and treat all knots with knotting, which seals the knots and prevents resin exuding. Leave to dry before beginning the next stage.

5. Lightly sandpaper the work, remove all dust and apply one coat of priming paint.

6. When dry, fill all nail holes and other small defects with putty, or with a powder filler such as Polyfilla or Alabastine.

7. Rub down once again with sandpaper and brush off dust.

8. Apply undercoat and leave to dry. One undercoat is advised for average work; two for work requiring a high quality finish. For good results lightly rub down with sandpaper between each coat.

9. Apply one coat of hard gloss paint. For a first-class finish on painted furniture, rub down with wet and dry abrasive paper between coats. It always pays to read carefully the manufacturers' instructions on paint and other products being used. Remember that brushes are tools, and should be well looked after. After use, wash them out in turps substitute and store flat.

Nails, Screws and Fittings

NAILS

Nails are used for fixing or holding wood or other suitable materials together, or when particular joints need strengthening. They are sold by weight. The larger headed nails such as French or wire nails are used for fencing, packing-case making, and for jobs where good holding power and not appearance is essential. Nails with small heads, such as panel pins and oval wire, are used where the fixing must be inconspicuous. Various types of nails in common use are illustrated in Fig. 27.

Fig. 27. Nails and screws. A : lost-head wire nail, B : oval wire nail, C : French or wire nail, D : panel pin, E : cut tack, F : sprig, G : head of Pozidriv screw, H : countersunk head screw, J : round screw, K : raised head screw, L and M : surface-type screw cup, N and O : flush-type screw cup

SCREWS

Screws are used for securing to wood fittings such as hinges, locks, bolts and handles. They are also used for reinforcing light framework, fixing tray bottoms, etc. Screws are usually known by the type of head and the kind of metal from which they are made. The three main types, as shown in Fig. 27, are (h) countersunk head, (j) round head, (k) raised head. The Phillips 'Pozidriv' wood screw is becoming increasingly popular in woodworking, and Fig. 27 shows a typical 'Pozidriv' screw head at (g). There are many different kinds of metal used in screw manufacture, the chief ones being steel, brass and silicon bronze. Screws can also be bright zinc plated, or made of nylon.

Sizes of screws are indicated by length and gauge, and when ordering it is necessary to state the number of screws required (remembering it

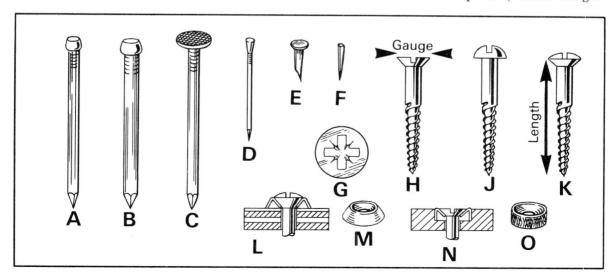

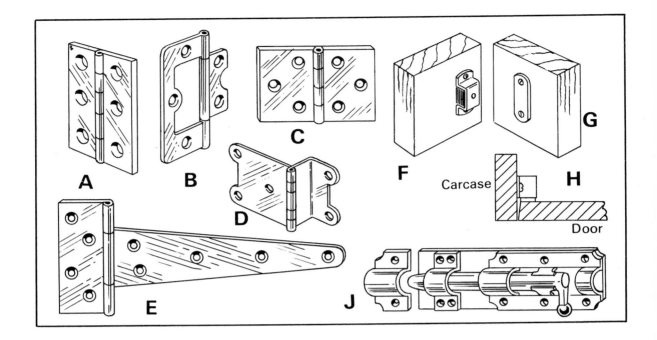

Fig. 28. Hinges and fittings. A : butt hinge, B : self-aligning 'Hurlinge', C : back flap hinge, D : kitchen cabinet hinge, E : tee hinge, F : magnetic cupboard catch, G : magnetic catch striker plate, H : magnetic catch closed position, J : tower bolt

is cheaper to buy by the gross), the length, the gauge, the type of head, the material, and the finish. For example, to fix two battens 19mm. ($\frac{3}{4}$in.) thick to a wall for shelf supports, you would probably need six 36mm. ($\frac{1}{2}$in.) No. 10 countersunk steel screws.

It is advisable to lubricate screws with a little petroleum jelly or tallow before driving in. Brass cups are used for neatness and on work where screws have to be removed occasionally (see Fig. 27 L and N).

FITTINGS

A wide variety of cabinet fittings is available for the woodworker. The prices of fittings vary considerably, so do not spoil a good job by using inferior quality goods. In the trade hinges for hanging doors are usually called butts, and brass butts (solid drawn) are widely used in cabinet making and joinery.

A selection of hinges and fittings is shown in

Figs. 28 and 29. Most used are:

Brass butts (solid drawn) A large range of sizes is available for doors, boxes, etc.

Back flaps The flanges are wide to provide a large surface area for screwing. They are suitable for table and desk flaps.

Self-aligning 'Hurlinge' These hinges are designed to make the fitting of hinges a simple and speedy operation and are now used widely in the building and furniture-making industries.

Kitchen cabinet hinge This is a cranked hinge, simple to fit, which does not require letting in.

Tee hinge Suitable for garden sheds, doors, etc., tee hinges usually have a black japanned finish.

Tower bolt Available in a large range of sizes, tower bolts are for securing French doors, gates, etc.

Magnetic cupboard catch Fig. 28F, G and H best explains the method of fixing.

Cupboard catch, plastic rocker type This catch is very good for securing small cabinet doors. The method of fixing is shown in Fig. 29A, B and C.

Ball catch This is a neat and effective door catch (see Fig. 29J, K and L).

Mirror plate A mirror plate is used for fixing bookcases, shelves, wall cabinets and mirrors (Fig. 29D).

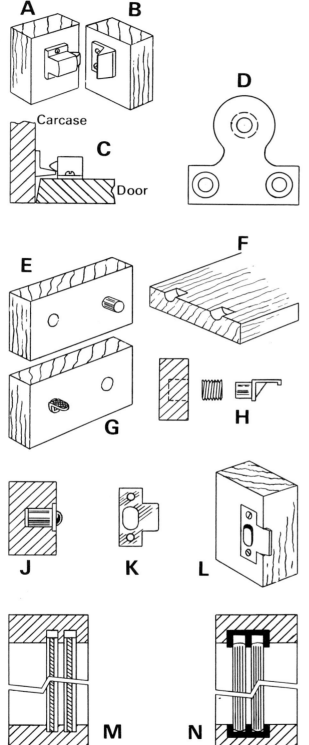

Track for glass or plywood doors Plywood or glass doors will run quite comfortably in plough grooves, worked on the cabinet. Note that the top grooves are made deeper to allow for the removal of the glass or plywood doors (see Fig. 29M). Fibre tracks suitable for glass doors are available in various sizes and qualities. For appearance they are better when let in.

Shelf supports Two simple methods of supporting shelves are shown in Fig. 29 at E and F and at G and H.

Fig. 29. *A further selection of fittings. A : plastic rocker catch, B : plastic rocker catch striker plate, C : plastic rocker catch closed position, D : mirror plate, E : adjustable shelf supporting by dowel rods, F : underside of shelf when using dowel rods, G : plastic shelf support, H : method of fitting plastic shelf support, J : ball catch, K : ball catch striking plate, L : ball catch striking plate fitted, M : plywood sliding doors in plough grooves, N : glass sliding doors in fibre track*

Practice and Simple Jobs

This chapter is designed to encourage the beginner, help him to understand the basic principles of marking out and the use of tools, and to get him used to working with and understanding woodworking materials. The abstract panels and sculpture described in this chapter are not only excellent for practice, but make attractive wall and table decorations in their own right.

ABSTRACT PANEL

The procedure for making the abstract panel shown in Figs. 30 and 31 is as follows:

1. Mark out the plywood panel, and with a tenon saw carefully cut 1mm. away from the line. This will leave you sufficient material to clean up the edges with a smoothing plane.

2. Mark out on cardboard and cut the number of squares you require for your design. Arrange these on the panel to form a pleasing pattern.

3. Mark out carefully all round the squares with a sharp grade H pencil. Drill a hole in a corner, and thread in a fret saw blade. With the fret saw carefully cut out the shape, remembering each cut-out piece is required for your picture.

4. Clean up the pieces you removed, and also the insides of the apertures with a fine-grade wood file and sandpaper.

5. Clean up panel and the cut-out shapes with No. $1\frac{1}{2}$ sandpaper. Wrap your sandpaper round a cork rubber or block of wood. Sandpaper held loosely in the fingers will spoil the edges of your work.

6. Lay the shapes in the position you have planned and mark lightly to locate for gluing.

7. Apply glue carefully to both surfaces, keeping within the location lines. If using impact adhesive, carefully lower the shapes on to the correct positions.

8. To finish, lightly polish the panel and cover the back with a harmonizing material from suitable furnishing fabrics or coloured hessian, etc.

Materials Required

1 piece of 6mm. mahogany-faced plywood, 300mm. × 200mm. Small piece of fabric for backing.

Tools

Rule, try square, marking knife, tenon saw, smoothing plane, wheelbrace and drill, fret saw, fine wood file, sandpaper and cork rubber.

FORM IN SCOTS PINE

Fig. 32 shows an abstract form in Scots pine and Fig. 33 the plan and elevations. Some parts of the form can be painted, and various harmonizing colours could be used to obtain different effects. Prepare your wood to the sizes given and follow the procedure notes below with Fig. 34.

1. Mark off length of form. Square all round at each end, using a try square and marking knife to obtain accuracy. When squaring all round make sure your try square is always in contact with a face side and a face edge.

2. Complete the setting out. Mark centres for boring holes, and gauge depth of housings and rebate at top of form.

3. Bore holes to take dowels, and make saw kerfs down to the gauge lines. Remember always to cut on the waste side of the line.

4. Remove waste from each side to form a ridge shape as shown in the drawing. Finish housing by chiselling carefully until flat—test frequently with a steel rule. Re-mark depth of side housings, and remove waste as before. Sandpaper form and glue in dowels. Attach base with two screws. Paint and polish as required.

Fig. 30. Abstract panel, designed for practice in marking out and sawing

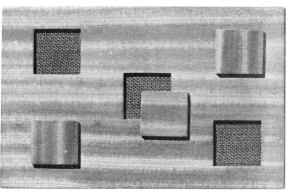

Fig. 31. Dimensions for abstract panel

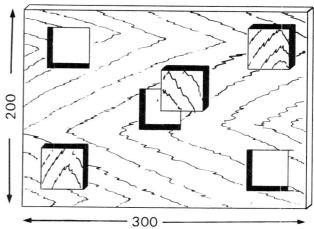

200

300

Fig. 32. Form in Scots pine

Fig. 33. Dimensions for form in Scots pine

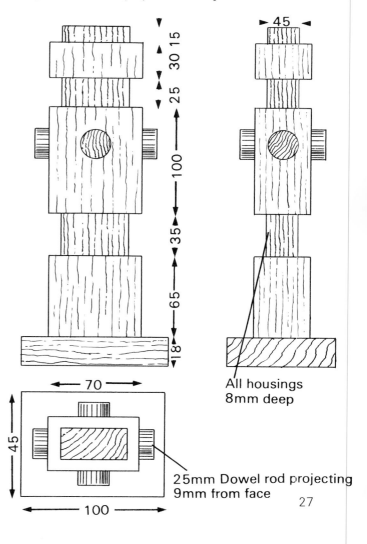

45

30 15

25

100

35

65

8

All housings
8mm deep

70

45

100

25mm Dowel rod projecting
9mm from face

27

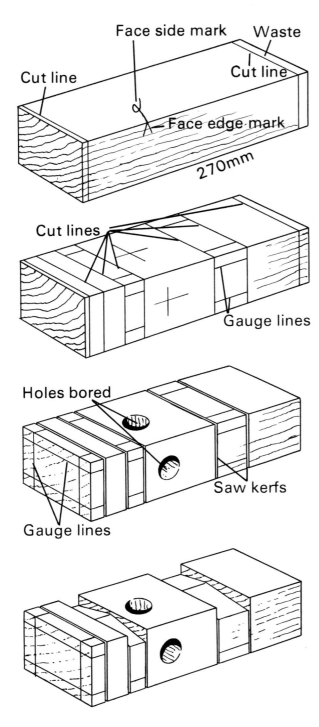

Face side mark Waste
Cut line Cut line
Face edge mark
270mm
Cut lines Gauge lines
Holes bored Saw kerfs
Gauge lines

Fig. 34. Operations in manufacture of Scots pine form

Materials Required

One piece of Scots pine of length 280mm., width 70mm., thickness 45mm. (finished sizes). Two 30mm. × No. 8 countersunk iron screws.

Tools

Smoothing plane, rule and try square, marking knife, marking gauge, brace and 25mm. (1in.) bit, tenon saw, 25mm. (1in.) and 18mm. ($\frac{3}{4}$in.) bevelled edged chisels, mallet and screwdriver.

SAWING TECHNIQUES

Maintain your saws in good condition, and sharpen them or have them sharpened regularly. A blunt saw can be dangerous. A bench hook is an important piece of equipment and is indispensible for supporting work when sawing or cleaning up shoulders, etc. This is an item that the home craftsman can usefully make for himself, and details for making one are given at the end of this chapter. Fig. 35 shows a method of sawing the shoulders of a housing. Note that the saw kerf must be kept on the waste side of the line; also that care must be taken not to saw below the gauge line, as this would weaken the job. Fig. 36 shows the sequence of cutting a tenon. The diagrams show quite clearly the saw kerf in the waste. Fig. 37 shows the cutting of a shoulder.

CHISELLING TECHNIQUES

Keep your chisels sharp. When chiselling, remember the safety rule: always keep the left hand behind the cutting edge. The chisel should be grasped easily but firmly, and in a horizontal paring the handle should bed comfortably in the palm, although sometimes it may be necessary to place the left hand over the blade.

Fig. 38A illustrates the method of holding the chisel when paring horizontally. The pressure of the thumb and forefinger helps to control the chisel. Fig. 38B illustrates the method of holding the chisel when paring vertically. Fig. 39 illustrates the method of chopping a mortise.

WALL PLAQUES

The plaques shown in Plate 2 can be hung vertically or horizontally. One is mounted on a hessian-covered plywood base, and selected facets are painted black, giving it a very pleasing appearance. The setting out, sawing and chiselling techniques already developed with the making of

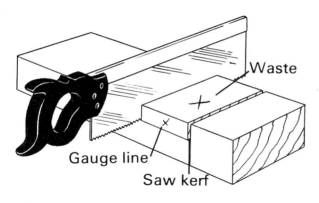

Fig. 35. Sawing the shoulders of a housing

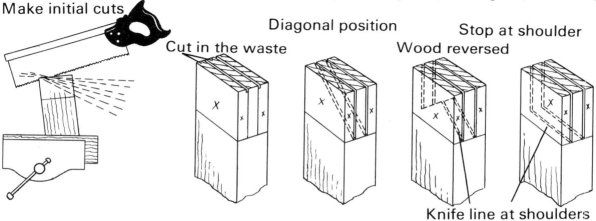

Fig. 36. Sequence of cutting a tenon
Fig. 37. Cutting a shoulder

the wood form can be applied to the plaques. The procedure for making the plaques is adequately shown in Fig. 40.

Material required for Plaque 1
One piece of Scots pine, of length 460mm.; width 95mm.; thickness 20mm. (finished sizes).

Material required for Plaque 2
One piece of Scots pine, of length 370mm.; width 85mm.; thickness 20mm. (finished sizes). One piece of plywood, of length 460mm.; width 125mm.; thickness 6mm. The hessian is paper backed and is glued on with 'Clam' or 'Copydex'.

Tools
Smoothing plane, rule, try square, marking gauge, marking knife, rebate plane, tenon saw, 25mm. (1in.) and 18mm. ($\frac{3}{4}$in.) paring chisels, mallet, router (for finishing housings).

The plaque in Columbian pine (Plaque 3, Fig. 40) is designed to give practice in the use of the plough. Various kinds of wood and metal can be inlaid in the plough grooves to make an attractive panel arrangement.

When using the plough to make the grooves, care is needed to prevent the plough iron tearing out possible cross grain. It is advisable to use a cutting gauge to mark out the grooves before proceeding with the ploughing.

Material required for Plaque 3
One piece of Columbian pine, of length 460mm.; width 95mm.; thickness 20mm. Odd lengths of wood and metal 6mm. × 6mm. for inlay.

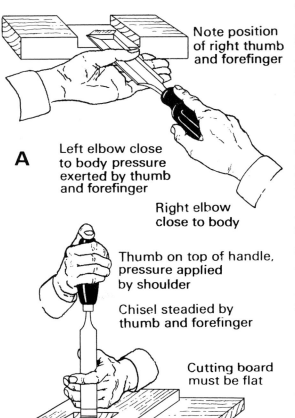

Note position of right thumb and forefinger

A

Left elbow close to body pressure exerted by thumb and forefinger

Right elbow close to body

Thumb on top of handle, pressure applied by shoulder

Chisel steadied by thumb and forefinger

Cutting board must be flat

Fig. 38. Paring with a chisel. A : horizontally, B : vertically

Fig. 39. Chopping a mortise

Tools
Smoothing plane, rule, try square, cutting gauge, plough and 6mm. cutter.

DOOR CONSTRUCTION
The door shown in Fig. 41A is of a simple flush type, consisting of a light frame made up of deal, 50mm. × 20mm. in section, and jointed with 6mm. diameter dowels. Plywood is glued to both sides of the frame, making a neat and attractive door. To conceal the edges of the plywood the door could be lipped all round with a 6mm. thick lipping. The dotted lines in Fig. 41A show how a larger door can be stiffened with extra rails.

JOINTS
The following are a range of simple joints suitable for light framing, tables, chairs, doors, etc.
Dowelling A dowelled joint if properly made is strong and reliable. Dowels can be purchased already made, or you can buy the dowel rod and make your own. Fig. 41B shows a simple and accurate method of marking out the dowel centres. Fine panel pins are driven in on one piece, and the heads are nipped off. The rail is then carefully positioned and pressed on to the pins, the indentation made giving the true centres for boring. The pins are withdrawn, and this clearly gives the centres on the stile. Note: all dowels required for framing must be grooved (Fig. 41C) —this allows the air to escape—and fitted hand tight only.

B *Halving Joint* A useful joint for light framing is a halving joint. Fig. 41D shows part of a frame with a halving joint glued and screwed together. One side of the frame is shown faced with ply-

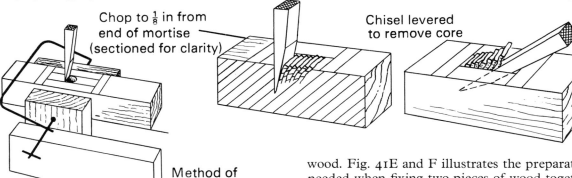

Chop to ⅛ in from end of mortise (sectioned for clarity)

Chisel levered to remove core

Method of holding material

wood. Fig. 41E and F illustrates the preparation needed when fixing two pieces of wood together with screws.
Bridle Joint Sometimes known as a slot mortise and tenon joint, widely used in light frame, chair and table construction. Fig. 42A shows a bridle

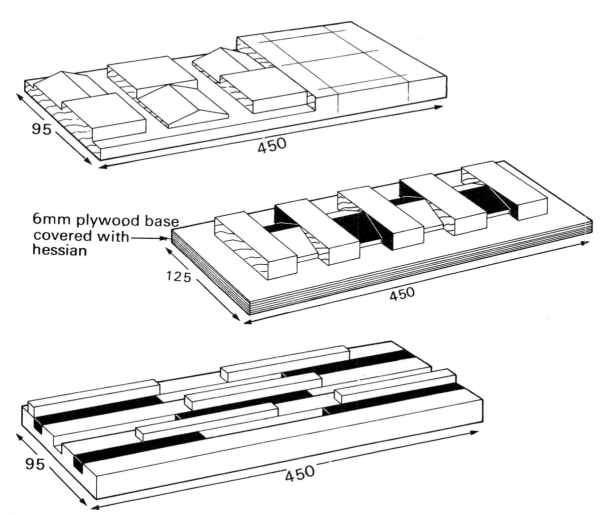

95
450

6mm plywood base
covered with
hessian

125
450

95
450

Fig. 40. Three wall plaques designed for practice in setting out, sawing and chiselling techniques

joint. Note that the tenon is approximately one-third of the rail thickness.

Through Mortise and Tenon Joint Fig. 42B shows a through mortise and tenon joint, a common woodwork joint widely used in various types of framing and construction. It is usually wedged for extra strength.

Haunched Mortise and Tenon Joint This is a joint used in framing, door construction, etc., where appearance and strength are important. A joint suitable for panelling and door construction is shown in Fig. 42F.

Through Dovetail Joint This is a joint suitable for framing and carcase work, and is shown ready for assembly in Fig. 42C. A dovetail template (see

Fig. 42D) is used to mark out the tails. The slope of the dovetail for hardwood is approximately 1 in 7, and for softwood it is approximately 1 in 6.

Lapped dovetail joint Used for framing and carcase work, a lapped dovetail joint is particularly useful for trays and drawer sides. Fig. 42E shows this joint assembled.

BENCH HOOK

The bench hook, sometimes called sawing block, is a piece of indispensible equipment and is easily made by the home craftsman. It is used to support the wood when sawing on the bench. It can be made in softwood, but beech will give much longer service. The bench hook can be used on either side. Fig. 43A shows details of construction.

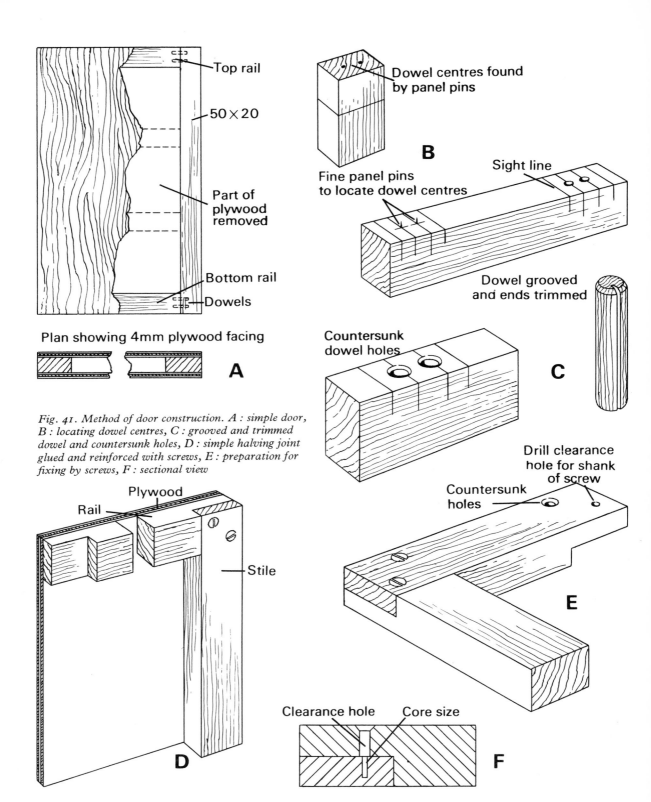

Top rail

50 × 20

Part of
plywood
removed

Bottom rail

Dowels

Plan showing 4mm plywood facing

A

Dowel centres found
by panel pins

B

Fine panel pins
to locate dowel centres

Sight line

Dowel grooved
and ends trimmed

Countersunk
dowel holes

C

*Fig. 41. Method of door construction. A : simple door,
B : locating dowel centres, C : grooved and trimmed
dowel and countersunk holes, D : simple halving joint
glued and reinforced with screws, E : preparation for
fixing by screws, F : sectional view*

Plywood

Rail

Stile

D

Drill clearance
hole for shank
of screw

Countersunk
holes

E

Clearance hole

Core size

F

32

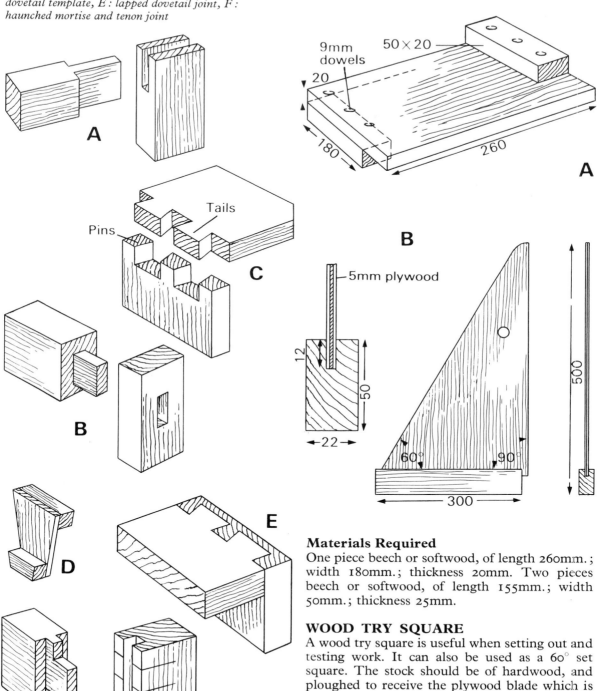

Fig. 42. A selection of joints. A : bridle joint, B : through mortise and tenon joint, C : through dovetail joint, D : dovetail template, E : lapped dovetail joint, F : haunched mortise and tenon joint

Fig. 43. Useful tools to be made. A : bench hook, B : wood try square

A

B

9mm dowels

50 × 20

20

180

260

Tails

Pins

C

B

B

D

E

F

5mm plywood

12

50

22

60°

90°

300

500

Materials Required

One piece beech or softwood, of length 260mm.; width 180mm.; thickness 20mm. Two pieces beech or softwood, of length 155mm.; width 50mm.; thickness 25mm.

WOOD TRY SQUARE

A wood try square is useful when setting out and testing work. It can also be used as a 60° set square. The stock should be of hardwood, and ploughed to receive the plywood blade which is glued in. Fig. 43B gives dimensions and details of construction.

33

Woodwork Projects

In this chapter details are given of 20 constructional projects which the home craftsman who has studied the preceding pages and obtained some practice should be able to tackle with considerable success.

NOTE ON POLISHING

The following applies to all the projects which are to be given a polished finish. It is advantageous to carefully clean up all inside surfaces of a job with sandpaper, and to polish these surfaces before gluing up. Precautions must be taken to keep the polish off the joint surfaces. This can be achieved by using masking tape on the shoulders and other parts of the locating surfaces. This technique not only makes the final polishing easier, but enables surplus glue to be cleaned off without difficulty.

1. OVENWARE STAND

Even in well-equipped modern kitchens, the melamine working surfaces need protection from very hot dishes and pans. This stand (see Plate 1) will give good protection and its size is adequate for most purposes. Made of teak, its warm brown colour and pleasant shape would enhance any kitchen or dining table. It will also look well and be quite serviceable if made in pine. The drawings (Fig. 44) give full dimensions and details of construction. The frame has a small chamfer— 3mm. × 3mm.—worked all round the top edges. A chamfer must be marked out with a pencil and thumb gauge. On no account should a marking gauge be used to mark out a chamfer, as this would damage the job. Fig. 44 shows the application and use of a thumb gauge.

Procedure

1. Prepare the material for the frame.
2. Mark out the sides (place together in pairs for accuracy) complete with the position of the slats.
3. Mark out the ends. Set a mortise gauge to suit a 9mm. firmer chisel and gauge the open mortise and bare-faced tenons, keeping the stock on the face edge of the frame. The exploded view shows this quite clearly.
4. Lay the frame out and number all joints. See the view showing construction.
5. Check all marking out before cutting any joints. Remember the rule: always cut in the waste. With a dovetail saw cut the tenon and open mortise.
6. Carefully cut the shoulders of the tenons, and with a firmer chisel remove the waste to complete the open mortise.
7. Fit joints and assemble the frame dry (that is without glue). Check the frame for wind.
8. Prepare material for the slats.
9. Remove waste on sides to make housings to take the slats and check for size. Fig. 35, page 29, shows the method of making housings.
10. Glue and pin frame, and check for squareness. Note: to prevent the wood splitting, bore small holes to take the panel pins.
11. Clean up slats and fit hand tight into housings.
12. Glue and pin slats in position, driving the pin heads lightly below the surface with a nail punch.
13. Allow glue to dry. Clean up frame and ends of slats.
14. Carefully round the corners of the frame as shown in plan.
15. Mark out the shaping on the sides and clean

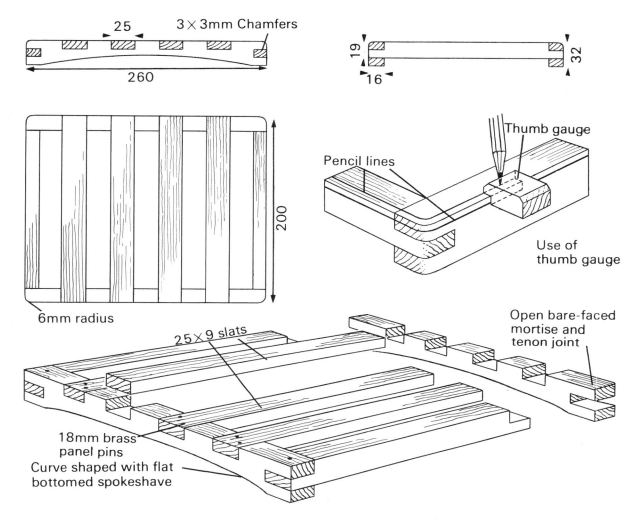

25
3 × 3mm Chamfers
260

19
16
32

200
6mm radius

25 × 9 slats

Thumb gauge
Pencil lines
Use of thumb gauge

Open bare-faced mortise and tenon joint

18mm brass panel pins
Curve shaped with flat bottomed spokeshave

Fig. 44. Drawings for ovenware stand

up with a flat-bottom spokeshave. Finish with sandpaper.

16. Mark out chamfers round top of stand with thumb gauge (see Fig. 44), and make chamfers with a block plane.

17. Clean up with sandpaper and finish the stand with a linseed oil mixture.

Materials Required

Teak or selected pine.

CUTTING LIST

Description	Length	Width	Thickness
Two sides	280mm.	32mm.	16mm.
Two ends	215mm.	19mm.	16mm.
Four slats	215mm.	25mm.	9mm.

Twelve 16mm. brass panel pins.

Tools

Jack and smoothing planes, rule, try square, marking gauge, tenon or dovetail saw, 9mm. firmer chisel, mortise gauge, mallet, 16mm. drill and small bit to suit panel pins, hammer, nail punch, thumb gauge (made from scrap piece of wood), flat-bottomed spokeshave, cork rubber and sandpaper.

2. BEDSIDE TABLE

The simplicity and ease of construction of this attractive table (Fig. 45) brings it well within the reach of the home craftsman. The table consists of two end frames, five pieces of dowel rod to form a shelf and a 16mm. Formica 'Beauty-board' top. As an alternative to the 'Beauty-board' top you could use 16mm. multi-plywood and face it with a Formica laminate to suit your own colour scheme or decor.

Plate 1. Ovenware stand (page 34) and cheese board with tiles (page 42)
Plate 2. Book rack (page 41) and three wall plaques (page 28)

The drawings (Fig. 46) give constructional details. Fig. 46A shows the through mortise and tenon joints connecting the bottom rails to the legs—note the saw kerfs made on the tenons and the wedges which are driven into the tenons when gluing up. The top rail is connected to the legs with a bridle joint. Fig. 46B shows an enlarged detail of bottom rail and location of dowel rods. It will be seen from this detail and the photograph that all the rails and legs are decorated with a 3mm. × 3mm. chamfer.

Procedure
1. Prepare the material to size.
2. Hold the four legs together and mark out the position of rails.
3. Hold together the two rails and mark out

Plate 3. *Magazine rack (page 44)*

Plate 4. *Two trays (page 45)*

Fig. 45. Bedside table

shoulders and length of tenons. Using a marking knife and try square, make a cut line round for the shoulders.

4. Set mortise gauge to a 9mm. mortise chisel and gauge all mortises. Note: owing to the small dimensions of the material an ordinary firmer chisel—not bevelled edged—could be used quite satisfactorily for chopping out the mortises.

5. Chop all mortises and cut tenons. Make saw kerfs in tenons of bottom rails.

6. Test for size and bore holes for dowel rods. Cut rods to correct length.

7. Fit end frames together and make adjustments as necessary.

8. Clean up all inside surfaces of the job with sandpaper, and polish these before gluing up. The dowels should all be polished before gluing up.

9. Prepare necessary sash cramps, and glue up end frames. Drive in the wedges carefully.

10. Clean up end frames (flush all joints and sandpaper) and drill holes in top rail for screws. Finish polishing.

11. Clean up and polish edges of top.

12. Glue ends of dowel rails and assemble table. Fix the top by screwing through the top rail of end frames.

Materials Required
Scots pine or Columbian pine.

16mm. multi-ply for top.
Formica to suit decor.

CUTTING LIST

Description	Length	Width	Thickness
Four legs	450mm.	37mm.	18mm.
Four rails	270mm.	37mm.	18mm.
Five dowel rods	340mm.	9mm. dia.	
Small piece of contrasting wood for wedges.			
One top	405mm.	290mm.	16mm.

Fig. 46. Drawings for bedside table. A and B show details of joints

(The top can be 'Beautyboard', or multi-ply with one piece of Formica).
Four 32mm. × No. 8 countersunk brass screws.

Tools

Jack and smoothing planes, rule, try square, marking gauge, mortise gauge, 9mm. firmer chisel, tenon or dovetail saw, mallet, brace and 9mm. dowel bit, wheelbrace and twist drill for No. 8 screws, screwdriver, hammer, cork rubber and sandpaper.

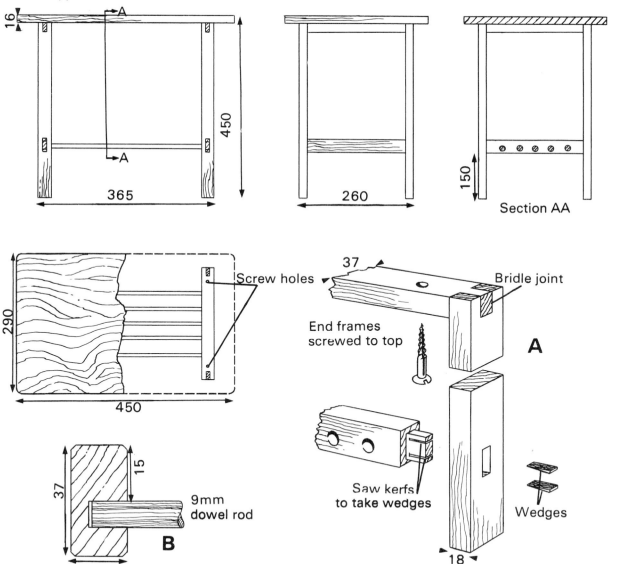

Plate 5. *Yew table (page 45)*   Plate 6. *Square table (page 47)*

3. BOOK RACK

In most homes space is at a premium, and this book rack or stand (Plate 2) has been designed to house those popular paperbacks we tend to accumulate.

The book rack is made in cedar wood. It is of simple construction and the base consists of two rails housed into the ends. The back also consists of two separate pieces which are shouldered and let into the ends. All joints are glued, and no nails or screws are needed as the rack is very strong when properly made. As an alternative, the bottom could be made in one piece, and the back made as one rail approximately 50mm. wide.

The design has a clean simple line which is pleasing in appearance. The end supports are rectangular in shape and have a small radius worked on the corners.

With a slight modification to size, this design can easily be converted into a rack to house spice jars. With two extra side rails let into the front, it also makes a rather nice plant stand. If you are making the plant stand, check size of the flower pots and alter dimensions to suit before cutting the material.

Procedure
1. Prepare all material.
2. Pair up the ends and mark out for back and bottom rails.
3. Make housings to receive the bottom rails. See Fig. 47A for the method of making a stopped housing. Make housings to take the back rails and shape ends.
4. Mark out the rails and cut joints.
5. Fit the bottom and back rails and assemble the job.
6. Clean up all inner surfaces and polish.
7. Glue up, test for squareness and leave to dry.
8. Clean up outer surfaces and complete polishing.

Materials Required
Pine, utile, oak, teak or cedar.

Fig. 47. Drawings for book rack. A shows the method of making a stopped housing

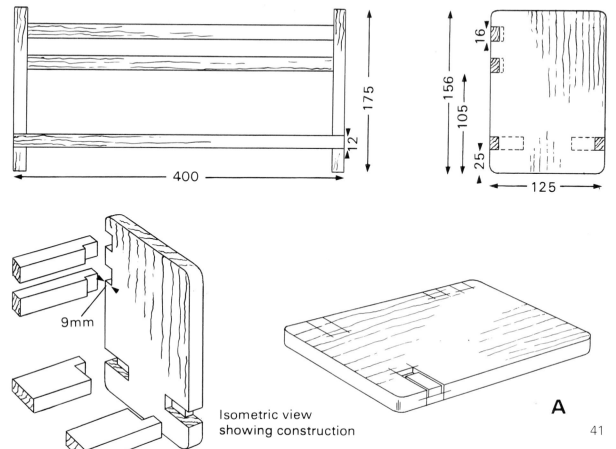

Isometric view
showing construction

A

41

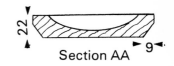

25

6

Section AA

22

9

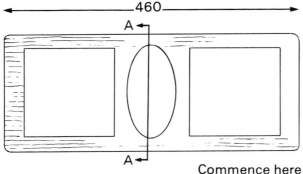

460

A

A

Commence here

Fig. 48. Drawings for cheese board. A shows the removal of waste

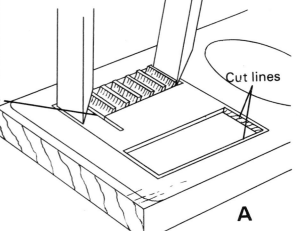

Cut lines

A

CUTTING LIST

Description	Length	Width	Thickness
Two ends	190mm.	125mm.	12mm.
Two bottom rails	410mm.	40mm.	12mm.
Two top rails	410mm.	16mm.	12mm.

Tools

Jack and smoothing planes, rule, try square, marking gauge, marking knife, dovetail saw, 9mm., 12mm., and 25mm. firmer chisels, mallet, block plane, cork rubber and sandpaper.

4. CHEESE BOARD WITH TWO TILES

This cheese board is of useful proportions. It has two 150mm. × 150mm. × 6mm. decorative ceramic tiles, and a centre portion which is carved out to make a small elliptical dish. The ends of the board are bevelled sufficiently to allow for easy lifting, and the sides are slightly bevelled for decoration. The board (shown in Plate 1 and Fig. 48) is made of teak, and the warm qualities of this wood, coupled with the decorative tiles, make this an attractive piece of tableware.

Other ideas might suggest themselves from this design, such as a tiled tray or shaped dishes.

Procedure

1. Prepare material to size.
2. Mark out the shape of board and the position of tiles. Make firm cut lines to locate the tiles on the board; this is achieved by making four gauge lines with the grain and four cut lines across the grain.
3. Cramp the job firmly to the bench and remove waste as shown in Fig. 48A. Finish to the correct depth with a router.
4. Try in tiles. Make the tiles a hand tight fit lengthwise of the grain and with a slight clearance on the width to allow for possible shrinkage.
5. Pencil in clearly the outline of the elliptical dish to be made in the centre of board. Carve out the waste (use a No. 6 carving gouge for this operation) and finish with sandpaper.
6. Cut the board to length and clean up the ends.
7. Mark out and make bevels on the ends and sides.
8. Clean up the board and glue in the tiles. If preferred they may be left loose.
9. To finish, wipe board over with olive oil and rub in well.

Materials Required

Sycamore, teak, utile or beech.

CUTTING LIST

Description	Length	Width	Thickness
One piece of teak	470mm.	200mm.	22mm.
Two ceramic tiles	150mm.	150mm.	6mm.

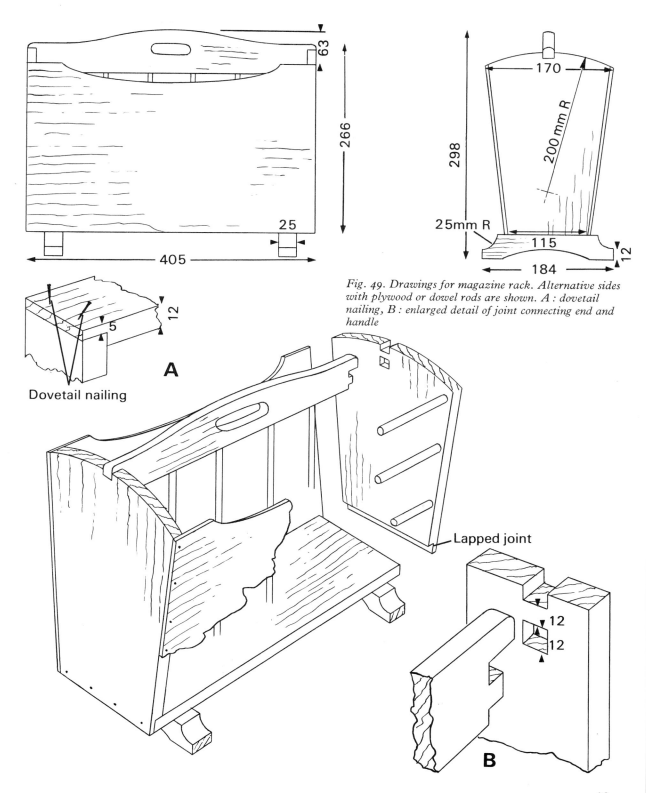

63

266

25

405

170

200 mm R

298

25mm R

115

12

184

12

Dovetail nailing

12

5

12

A

Fig. 49. Drawings for magazine rack. Alternative sides with plywood or dowel rods are shown. A : dovetail nailing, B : enlarged detail of joint connecting end and handle

Lapped joint

12

12

B

Plate 7. *Bedside cabinet (page 48) and upholstered dressing stool (page 69)*
Plate 8. *Sewing box (page 50)*

Tools
Jack and smoothing planes, winding strips, rule, try square, marking gauge, marking knife, 18mm. and 25mm. firmer chisels, mallet, router, tenon saw, cabinet scraper, 12mm. No. 6 carving gouge, cork rubber and sandpaper.

5. MAGAZINE RACK
For the busy housewife, a receptacle to hold the various current newspapers, weekly and monthly periodicals is a necessity.

The simplicity of design and construction of the magazine rack illustrated in Plate 3 will appeal to the home craftsman. It consists mainly of a base, two shaped ends, a handle for lifting, four dowel rods to make the centre division, two pieces of plywood and two shaped feet.

The ends are simply joined to the base with lapped joints which are glued and pinned. The pins are driven in dovetail fashion as shown in Fig. 49A. The shaped handle is stub-tenoned into the ends (see Fig. 49B). Note the housings made on top of the ends to prevent the handle from twisting. Variations would be to replace the plywood sides with dowel rods or to apply a painted finish.

Procedure
1. Prepare all material.
2. Shape the ends and make lapped joints.
3. Shape the handle, cut out the hand holes and make tenon on ends.
4. Cut mortises on ends to receive the handle, and assemble dry.
5. Bore holes for dowel rods in base and handle rail. Cut dowel rods to length.
6. Try up (dry) the base, ends, dowels, and handle. Make adjustments as necessary. Clean up all inside faces, and polish.
7. Glue up base, ends, dowels and handle. Nail lapped joints (Fig. 49A) and leave to dry.
8. Cut plywood sides to shape, glue and nail to ends and base. Punch nail heads slightly below the surface and fill up holes with Polyfilla shaded to match the colour of the wood.
9. Clean up all round and complete polishing.
10. Shape the feet, polish and screw to base.

Materials Required
Parana pine, for base, ends and feet. 4mm. mahogany-faced plywood, for sides (or alternatively make base, ends and feet in utile).

CUTTING LIST

Description	Length	Width	Thickness
Base	415mm.	120mm.	12mm.
Two ends	275mm.	170mm.	12mm.
Handle rail	415mm.	63mm.	12mm.
Four pieces of dowel rod	250mm.	6mm. dia.	
Two feet	195mm.	32mm.	25mm.
Two sides (plywood)	415mm.	260mm.	4mm.

Eight 19mm. panel pins.
Twenty 16mm. panel pins.

Tools

Jack and smoothing planes, winding strips, rule, try square, marking gauge, marking knife, tenon saw, 9mm. and 25mm. firmer chisels, mallet, rebate plane, brace and 22mm., 8mm. and 6mm. twist bits, coping saw, wood file to finish handle, hammer, nail punch, cork rubber and sandpaper.

6. TRAYS

Trays are necessities in the home, and at party time an extra one or two are always useful. The two trays shown in Plate 4 are well proportioned and can easily be stored when not in use.

The tray illustrated in Fig. 50A is made of teak and has a Formica-faced plywood bottom rebated in and screwed to the framing. The ends are cut out to form the handles, and bridle joints are used for the framing. For comfort the handle aperture is rounded. This is shown quite clearly in the enlarged details of the end and the various sections. The main features of the tray shown in Fig. 50B are the shaped ends (forming handles), the bottom, which is rebated in and screwed, and the finger joints. The enlarged detail shows the small nib which fits into and fills up the rebate.

Procedure

For making the tray shown in Fig. 50B:
1. Prepare all material.
2. Make a cardboard template of one end.
3. Mark out the ends (use template for this). With a coping or pad saw, cut out the top shaping of the handle and clean up. Remove the handle aperture with coping saw after rebating for bottom.
4. Set the mortise gauge and mark out finger joints on ends and sides. Gauge for rebate to take bottom.

5. Make the rebate and cut the finger joints.
6. Fit the joints and assemble dry.
7. Clean up and polish the inner surface and glue up framing. Two sash cramps are useful for this operation. Test for squareness and leave to dry.
8. Prepare the bottom. Face with veneer or Formica as required.
9. Fit in the bottom. Mark out for screws, drill holes and screw in bottom.
10. Complete polishing.

Materials Required

Tray 1: Teak framing with coloured Formica on plywood bottom.

CUTTING LIST (TRAY 1)

Description	Length	Width	Thickness
Two sides	470mm.	28mm.	8mm.
Two ends	320mm.	28mm.	8mm.
One bottom, plywood	465mm.	315mm.	
One piece of Formica	465mm.	315mm.	

Tray 2: Walnut or oak framing, with walnut veneer or Formica on plywood bottom.

CUTTING LIST (TRAY 2)

Description	Length	Width	Thickness
Two sides	470mm.	32mm.	11mm.
Two ends	320mm.	48mm.	11mm.
One bottom plywood	465mm.	315mm.	5mm.
One piece of veneer or Formica	465mm.	315mm.	

Eighteen 12mm. × No. 4 countersunk brass screws.

Tools

Jack and smoothing planes, rule, try square, marking gauge, mortise gauge, marking knife, dovetail saw, coping or pad saw, spokeshave, 6mm. and 25mm. firmer chisels, mallet, rebate plane, wood file and rasp, wheelbrace and twist drill, bradawl, screwdriver, cork rubber and sandpaper.

7. YEW TABLE

This table (see Plate 5) consists of a slab of 45mm. thick yew wood and four turned legs. Where no lathe is available, the legs may be made square and will look equally attractive.

Fig. 50. Drawings for trays

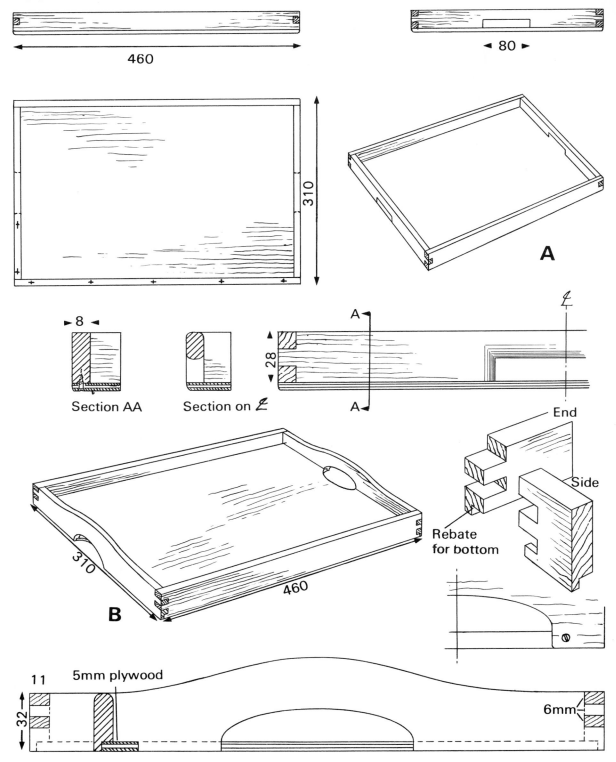

460

◄ 80 ►

310

A

► 8 ◄

28

Section AA   Section on ∠

A

A

End

Side

Rebate
for bottom

310   460

B

11   5mm plywood

32

6mm

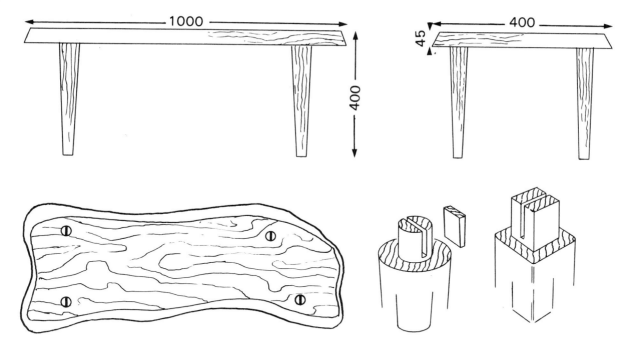

Fig. 51. Drawings for yew table. Alternative legs (round or square) are shown in detail. Dimensions are a guide to a suitable size

A tenon or spigot is made on the legs, and these go through the top and are securely wedged. Slab material of the kind suitable for this type of table can be found in most hardwood specialist timber yards. Slab material is also available in elm. Yew can be beautifully marked and full of interesting knots and irregular shapes; it is worth searching for. When you have found a suitable slab, leave it to dry out slowly in a dry, sheltered spot. When it is dry you can begin working on it.

Procedure

1. Prepare the legs. If turned, leave a spigot or circular tenon of 25mm. diameter. If the legs are made square, make a 25mm. square tenon and mortise into the top.
2. Prepare the top, clean with a sharp jack plane and test for winding.
3. Cut to length and shape the ends to blend in with the general contours of your piece of yew.
4. Mark out the position of the legs, and bore holes to take the spigot, or mortise for square tenon.
5. Fit in the legs and assemble the table dry.
6. Clean up the top using a sharp smoothing plane and scraper.

7. Cut the wedges—a contrasting wood makes a pleasant finish.
8. Glue up, drive in wedges and make flush when dry.
9. Sandpaper and give the top and legs a linseed oil finish.

Materials Required
Yew or elm.

CUTTING LIST

Description	Length	Width	Thickness
One top	1000mm.	400mm.	35 to 45mm.
Four legs	420mm.	45mm.	45mm.
Four wedges			

Tools
Jack and smoothing planes, tenon saw, bow saw, Surform files, spokeshave, brace and 25mm. twist bit, 18mm. firmer chisel, mallet, hammer, cabinet scraper, sandpaper.

8. SQUARE TABLE
The mahogany veneered blockboard top and sectional legs and rails in the contrasting Columbian pine gives this table an unusual and distinctive look (see Plate 6).

Laminboard and blockboard tops are usually lipped to conceal the end grain. In this design the end grain has been deliberately used as a decorative feature, and the slats are housed in the rails to give a complementary effect. Naturally, as good a piece of blockboard as possible should be obtained, but if there are any gaps between the blocks these can be filled with wedges. All joints —other than the slats—are dowelled. The technique of dowelling should be carefully studied (see page 30).

The table consists of two side frames, two wide end rails, four slats and a top, which is fixed by pocket screwing (Fig. 52A). Small blocks to take the screws may be glued to the top rail, as in Fig. 52B.

Procedure

1. Prepare the material.
2. Hold the four legs either in a vice or with 'G' cramps, and work out the rail positions and dowel locations complete with panel pins.
3. Mark out (use marking knife) and cut to length the four side rails. Clean up ends on shooting board, as shown in Fig. 53.
4. Locate rails for one frame and press on to pins. Number for ease of identification. Bore holes for dowels in rails and legs. Repeat for second frame.
5. Make chamfers on rails, cut out housings for slats, clean up inner surfaces and polish.
6. Dowels should be hand tight only; do not force in with hammer. Glue up, check for square and leave to dry.
7. Clean up and polish side frames.
8. Mark out the wide end rails, locate on side frame, and bore holes for dowels. Try up dry.
9. Make pockets for screws in the top rails, or glue on blocks.
10. Polish the end rails and glue up the table.
11. Clean up and polish the top. Fix to rails.
12. Cut slats to length and rebate ends to form shoulder.
13. Clean up, polish and glue in slats.
14. Using a block plane, complete chamfering on the ends of the slats. Make a small chamfer all round the bottom of the legs; this prevents damage to the leg at floor level.

Materials Required
Columbian pine for table framing.
Mahogany-faced blockboard for top.

CUTTING LIST

Description	Length	Width	Thickness
Four legs	400mm.	47mm.	22mm.
Four side rails	480mm.	47mm.	22mm.
Two end rails	510mm.	85mm.	22mm.
Four slats	540mm.	37mm.	16mm.
One top, blockboard	560mm.	560mm.	16mm.
One piece of dowel rod	1,200mm.	8mm. dia.	

Six 31mm. × No. 8 countersunk brass screws.

Tools
Jack and smoothing planes, block plane, winding strips, two 760mm. sash cramps, rule, try square, marking gauge, marking knife, brace and 8mm. twist bit, 25mm. firmer chisel, mallet, tenon saw, cabinet scraper, screwdriver, bradawl, cork rubber and sandpaper.

9. BEDSIDE CABINET
This useful cabinet (Plate 7) is of simple construction, good proportions and takes up very little space. It also has a number of unusual design features, mainly (a) the back of the cabinet is finished similarly to the front, and if required it can be used as an occasional table; (b) it is easily converted into a cupboard, by making a rebate or a plough groove to accommodate a back, and making and fitting a flush or panelled door; (c) if required a small drawer could be fitted.

The carcase is through-dovetailed at the top, and the end grain of the pins and tails—when neatly executed—give a very pleasing effect. The marking out of the dovetails is shown in Fig. 54A. The pins are arranged in this manner to accentuate the chamfers and corner treatment. The middle shelf is stopped-housed to the sides. The bottom shelf is connected to the sides with through circular tenons. These tenons are wedged with a contrasting wood. With a slight modification to the design, the construction could be further simplified, as is shown in Fig. 54B.

Procedure
1. Prepare all material.
2. Mark out the top for dovetailing, and cut tails.
3. Mark out the ends in pairs. Cut pins and fit dovetails.
4. Mark out the positions of circular tenons on the sides and bore the 14mm. holes; bore from each side to prevent splitting, keeping the bit at right angles to the wood.

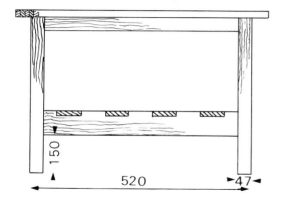

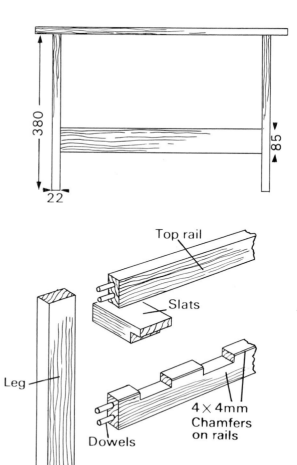

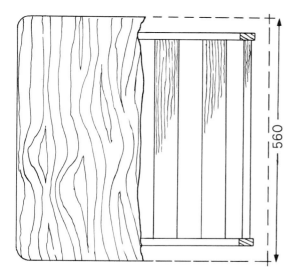

Fig. 52. Drawings for square table. A : pocket screwing, B : how the top is fixed by screwing into blocks

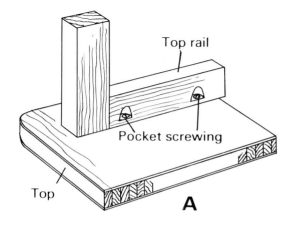

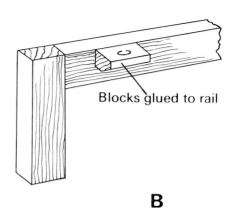

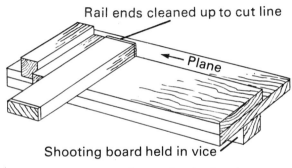

Rail ends cleaned up to cut line

← Plane

Shooting board held in vice

Fig. 53. Cleaning up ends on a shooting board

5. Cut stopped housings for bottom and top shelf, finishing to correct depth with a router.

6. Cut and fit shelf.

7. Fit the bottom shelf into the housing, and with an awl mark round the inside of the holes to give position of circular tenons. Bevel bottom edges of both shelves (see Fig. 54).

8. Cut tenons square, removing the waste between with a bow or pad saw. Make the tenons round with a fine wood rasp. Fit tenons and test for squareness. Make saw kerf for wedges—note the direction of saw kerf.

9. Bow-saw or pad-saw legs to shape. Clean up and make all chamfers.

10. Clean up the inside surfaces for polishing.

11. Cut wedges, prepare cramping pieces (to prevent bruising, blocks of wood are placed under cramp heads) and sash cramps. Glue up. Test for squareness, glue and carefully drive in wedges.

12. Flush all joints and complete chamfering.

13. Finish with French polish or wax.

Materials Required

Utile, oak, teak or pine.

CUTTING LIST

Description	Length	Width	Thickness
Two sides	610mm.	225mm.	16mm.
One top	390mm.	225mm.	16mm.
One bottom	390mm.	225mm.	16mm.
One shelf	380mm.	225mm.	16mm.

Tools

Jack and smoothing planes, winding strips, rule, try square, marking gauge, marking knife, marking awl, brace and 14mm. twist bit, 9mm., 12mm. firmer chisels, dovetail template, mallet, tenon saw, dovetail saw, coping saw, bow saw, wood file, scraper, cork rubber and sandpaper.

10. SEWING BOX

This attractive sewing box is planned to accommodate the usual necessities for needlework requirements. The box shown in Plate 8 is made of mahogany veneered blockboard. It has framed legs of rosewood, which are secured to the box with screws from the inside. The lids are arranged to open out to form a useful working surface. The commodious interior is fitted with a sliding tray which is divided into sections for equipment. Three dowel rods are positioned to provide adequate space for a good range of cotton reels, so that the colours can be seen at a glance. The box carcase is jointed together with five 8mm. diameter dowels down each side corner joint. The lids are hinged with good-quality piano hinge. Section AA in Fig. 55 shows clearly the provision made for tray and lid arrangement.

Procedure

1. Prepare all material.

2. Mark out sides and ends.

3. Cut to shape and fit lipping on edges. Note the handle cut out which is on one side; this is to be lipped. Glue on lipping and leave to dry.

4. Mark out the dowel locations and bore holes. Take care to check the depth of holes in the sides; do not spoil the job by coming through the side with a twist bit.

5. Work stopped plough groove on sides and ends to take the plywood bottom.

6. Cut hinging pieces to length and dowel to sides.

7. Cut the bottom to size and fit.

8. Clean up all the inner surfaces, cut dowels to length and try up carcase dry. Make adjustments as necessary.

9. Glue up (all cramps and blocks should be at hand and ready to use before the glue is applied) and leave to dry.

10. Mark out and cut the lids, let in hardwood for finger grip, and lip edges.

11. Polish and hinge the lids.

12. Mark out and shape legs. Make bridle joints.

13. Glue up legs. When dry complete the polishing and screw the legs to the carcase.

14. Fit tray slides and glue to the sides.

15. Make and fit the tray. Finger or dovetail joints may be used for the tray. The bottom can either be rebated in or simply glued and planted on.

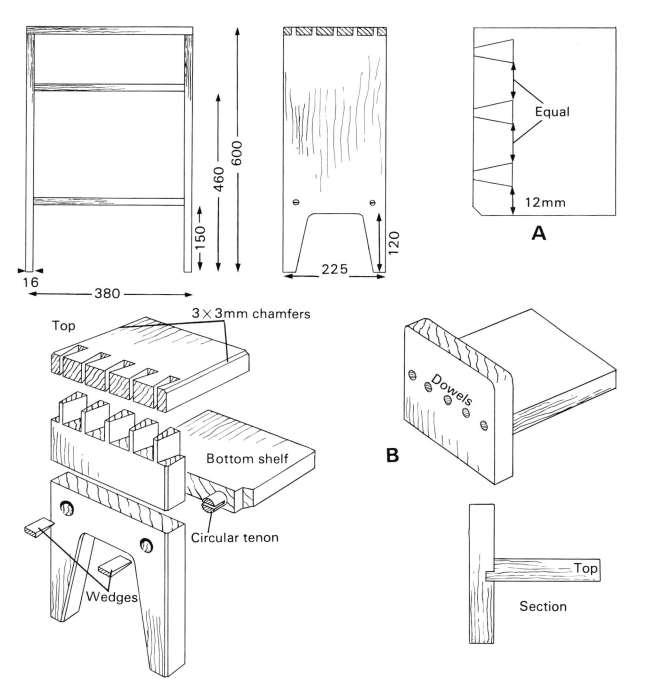

Fig. 54. Drawings for bedside cabinet. A : marking out dovetails, B : simplified tongued and grooved and dowelled joint for shelves

Materials Required

Mahogany-faced blockboard for carcase.
Walnut or rosewood for legs.
Sycamore for tray.

CUTTING LIST

Description	Length	Width	Thickness
Two sides	500mm.	270mm.	16mm.
Two ends	280mm.	260mm.	16mm.
Two lids	280mm.	200mm.	16mm.
Two hinging pieces	280mm.	45mm.	16mm.

Plate 9. Coffee table (page 60)

Four pieces of lipping	800mm.	18mm.	6mm.
Four pieces of lipping	500mm.	18mm.	6mm.
One bottom, Plywood	440mm.	300mm.	6mm.
Four legs	330mm.	32mm.	22mm.
Two rails	310mm.	32mm.	16mm.
Two pieces for tray	600mm.	40mm.	6mm.
One piece for tray division	600mm.	40mm.	6mm.
Two drawer runners	480mm.	11mm.	8mm.
One piece for handles	140mm.	36mm.	18mm.

Ten 25mm. × No. 8 countersunk brass screws.

Tools

Jack and smoothing planes, block plane, plough plane, rule, try square, marking gauge, marking knife, tenon saw, dovetail saw, brace and 8mm. twist bit, 25mm. and 6mm. firmer chisels, mallet, 9mm. scribing gouge for shaping handles, wheelbrace and drills, cabinet scraper, cork rubber and sandpaper.

11. CANDLE HOLDERS

Wood laminating is an interesting technique of bending and shaping thin strips or laminations of wood on formers or jigs. On removal from the jig very little attention is necessary, apart from cleaning up the edges and preparing for polishing. The article retains its shape and saves hours of cutting out and shaping. The technique has the added advantage of eliminating short grain. The lamination must be cut out of straight-grained timber, and glued up with a resin type of glue. Some suitable woods for bending are beech, ash, sycamore, teak, American elm, oak and utile.

These attractive candle holders make a pleasing table decoration, particularly when entertaining to dinner. The holder is made up of four laminations, consisting of two laminations of mahogany and two of beech. Other combinations of woods can be used.

Procedure

1. Make a full-size drawing of the former, and mark out the position of the four laminations. The small cramping block must be shaped to fit the bottom lamination.
2. Make the former to the dimensions given in Fig. 56. Beech is an excellent material for jigs or formers, but a softwood former is quite suitable for the production of a limited number of candle

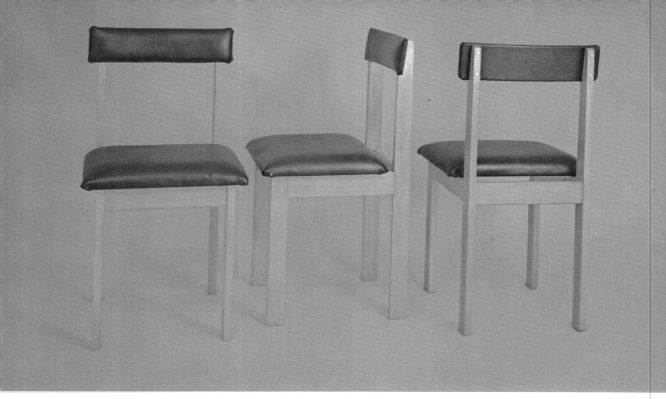

Plate 10. Three views of dining chair (page 57)

Plate 11. Dining table (page 55) with two dining chairs (page 57)

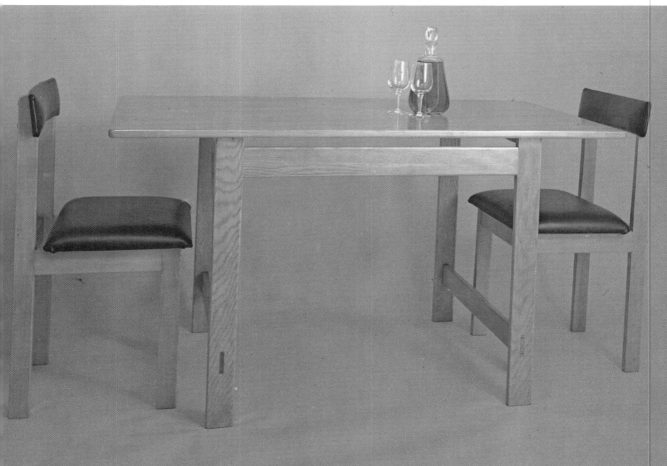

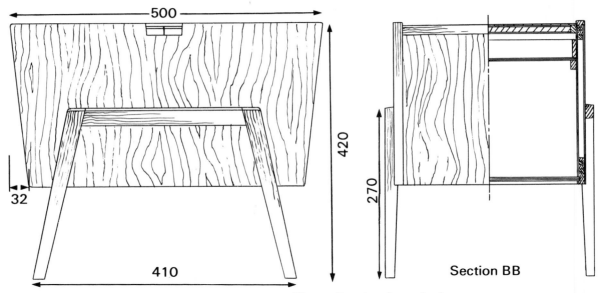

500

420

270

32

410

Fig. 55. Drawings for sewing box

Section BB

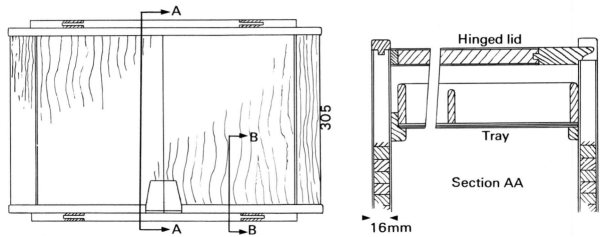

A

B

A

B

305

Hinged lid

Tray

Section AA

16mm

holders. The jig serves a dual purpose. It is used when gluing up the laminations, and also for boring the 11mm. diameter holes. Cut out the shape with a bow saw, and clean up with flat- and round-bottom spokeshaves.

3. Cut the laminations to size, place in the former and cramp up dry. Note the piece of rubber webbing used as a pressure pad. This takes up any small discrepancies.

4. Rub candle grease over the cramping surfaces of the jig. Apply resin glue to the laminations and cramp up. Check for alignment. Wipe off surplus glue and leave to dry.

5. Remove from the jig and saw to length. Replace and cramp up in vice. Clean edges and finish to width. Bore the holes to accommodate

the candles, using the jig to locate them.

6. Shape holder as required, and clean up with sandpaper and polish.

Materials Required

Utile, sycamore or ramin.

CUTTING LIST

Description	Length	Width	Thickness
Jig, one piece	300mm.	60mm.	40mm.
Laminations, four pieces	220mm.	40mm.	3mm.

Tools

See list at end of next project: 'Bracket for Wall Light'.

12. BRACKET FOR WALL LIGHT

Wall lights make a charming addition to the decor of a room. The wall bracket illustrated in Fig. 57 consists of a shaped base to which is tenoned a laminated bracket to hold the lamp fitting.

Procedure

1. Prepare a full-size working drawing of the bracket. The laminations are tapered towards the lamp fitting and allowance must be made for this on the former.
2. Mark out the former to the given dimensions, bow-saw to shape and clean up with spokeshave.
3. Taper laminations and cut off to jig lengths. Insert laminations and cramp up dry.
4. To prevent the job adhering to the former, rub candle grease over the cramping surfaces. Apply resin glue to the laminations and locate in jig. Place pressure pad and set off paper along one side of former. Cramp up and wipe off surplus glue. Leave to dry.
5. Remove cramps, clean up and level edges. This can be done successfully by holding together the former and the job in the vice. Mark out the length of the job and cut tenon. Cut bracket to length and round edge. Bore holes for the flex and clean up for polishing.
6. Mark out the base, cut mortise and fit bracket. Bore holes in the back and make slots for fixing.
7. Shape base and work chamfers. Clean up and polish.
8. Glue in bracket and leave to dry. Bore the hole for flex in base. Screw on brass nipple, wire up and fix lampholder.

Materials Required

Utile is suggested for the base, with utile and ash contrasting laminations.

CUTTING LIST

Description	Length	Width	Thickness
One base	160mm.	85mm.	22mm.
Seven pieces, for laminations	200mm.	28mm.	3mm.
One piece, for former	220mm.	100mm.	32mm.
One brass nipple and screws.			
One lampholder.			

Tools

The following tools are required for both candle holder and wall bracket.

Jack and smoothing planes, bow saw, flat- and round-bottom spokeshaves, tenon saw, brace, 11mm. and 9mm. twist bits, wheelbrace and twist drills, 5mm. and 25mm. firmer chisels, wood rasp, sandpaper.

13. DINING TABLE

The special features of this dining table (see Plate 11) make it particularly attractive to those setting up home on a limited budget. These are its pleasing appearance, useful proportions and economy of material, coupled with its ease of construction. The next project is a dining chair, designed to match the table, so the reader can make the whole suite. Two of the chairs are shown with the table in Plate 11. Although this table was designed to be made in Columbian pine, it would look equally good if made in a suitable hardwood.

Procedure

1. Prepare all material, select and match the grain.
2. Mark out the end frames, and cut dovetails on top rails.
3. Cut tenons on lower rails and chop mortise in legs (see Fig. 58A). Note the position of saw kerfs to take wedges.
4. Mark out and cut pins at top of legs and fit top end rails. See lapped dovetail joint, Fig. 58B.
5. Try up end frames dry. Clean up all inside surfaces, make mouldings (see sections) on bottom rails. Complete sandpapering as required and polish.
6. Mark out the side rails, cut tenons and chop mortises. Fig. 58B shows the setting out and location of the mortises to receive side rails.

Fig. 56. Drawings for laminated candle holders

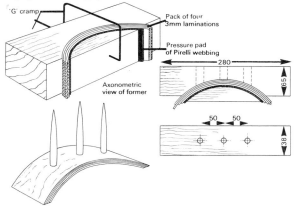

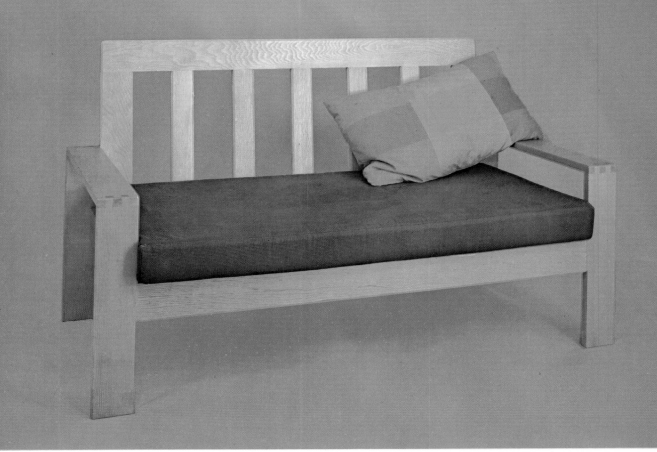

Plate 12. Settee without back cushion (page 60)

7. Glue up and wedge the end frames, test for squareness and leave to dry. Flush all joints and prepare for polishing.

8. Assemble table up dry, and make adjustments as necessary. Note: if fitting a solid top to the table, provision must be made for shrinkage. To cater for possible movement, slots are made to take the screws in the top rails of the end framing. This arrangement is shown clearly in Fig. 58C and in the plan of the table.

9. Make slots in top rails and glue up table frame. Test for squareness and leave to dry. Flush all joints and complete polishing.

10. Match and arrange the grain of the top to the best advantage and joint up top. Square-edge jointing is quite satisfactory, although for extra strength the joints may be stiffened with dowels; about five along each joint would be sufficient.

11. Glue up top, and when dry flush all joints and carefully clean up using a sharp smoothing plane and scraper. Shape corners and mould edges as shown in drawing.

12. Carefully sandpaper top and complete polishing. Fix top on table framing with twelve 35mm. × No. 10 countersunk screws.

Materials Required

Columbian pine, chestnut or oak. For an alternative top, oak-faced blockboard can be used with lipped edges.

CUTTING LIST

Description	Length	Width	Thickness
Five pieces to make top	1310mm.	145mm.	22mm.
Four legs	740mm.	70mm.	22mm.
Four end rails	670mm.	70mm.	22mm.
Two side rails	800mm.	70mm.	22mm.

Tools

Trying, jack and smoothing planes, shoulder plane, winding strips, rule, try square, marking gauge, marking knife, mortise gauge, 9mm. sash mortise chisel, mallet, dovetail template, tenon saw, hand saw, 18mm., 9mm. and 6mm. firmer chisels, cabinet scraper, wheelbrace and drills, cork rubber and sandpaper, screwdriver, hammer, two 1000mm. sash cramps.

14. DINING CHAIR

This chair (Plate 10) is made in Columbian pine with black cirrus vinyl covering material; this gives a pleasant colour combination. It is designed to be used with the dining table described in the previous project, the table and two of the chairs being shown in Plate 11. Its main features are the side frames which are mortised and tenoned, or dowelled jointed. The side frames are connected with a front and back rail, and the plywood seat base and upholstered back gives additional support.

The back rail is made up of three pieces of 4mm. plywood (see detail in Fig. 59). The seat base is of 122mm. plywood. It is necessary to bore holes into this to provide ventilation trim for the upholstery. The chairs and the table in

Plate 13. Settee with back cushion (page 60)

Plate 11 are finished with two coats of white French polish, rubbed down, and finally waxed.

Procedure
1. Prepare all material.
2. Mark out back and front legs in pairs (handed) showing position of mortises, floor line and total height of chair.
3. Mark out the side, back and front rails.
4. Set mortise gauge to an 8mm. sash mortise chisel, and gauge all mortises and tenons.
5. Cut mortises and tenons, and assemble side frames. Test for wind and adjust as necessary.
6. Clean up inner surfaces and glue up side frames. When dry, flush all joints.

Note: The former to shape the back rail is made out of a piece of deal 460mm. × 100mm. × 50mm. which is dished 18mm. deep. This dishing is shown in an enlarged detail in Fig. 59. See also the former for the candleholder shown in Fig. 56.
7. Prepare three pieces of 4mm. plywood to make

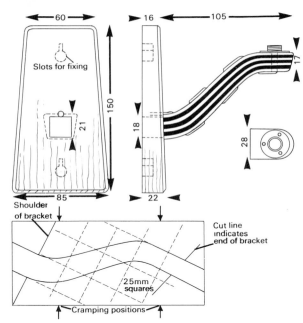

Fig. 57. Drawings for bracket for wall lights

shaped back rail and glue up in former. This technique is known as formed plywood. When dry, remove from former, cut to length and complete shaping.

8. Fit the front and back rails. Cut out seating at top of the legs to receive shaped back rail and drill for screws.

9. Glue and screw seat blocks on the side framing (see enlarged details in Fig. 59).

10. Prepare cramps and cramping blocks and glue in front and back rails. Test the chair for squareness and leave to dry.

11. Clean up and complete polishing.

12. Prepare the seat base; bore ventilating holes. Screw base to chair frame.

13. Screw on shaped back rail.

14. Remove back rail and seat base and prepare for upholstery work.

CUTTING LIST

Description	Length	Width	Thickness
Two back legs	820mm.	47mm.	22mm.
Two front legs	430mm.	47mm.	22mm.
Two side rails	390mm.	65mm.	22mm.
One front rail	350mm.	65mm.	22mm.
One back rail	350mm.	65mm.	22mm.
Two seat bearers	290mm.	25mm.	25mm.
Three pieces of plywood for shaped back	420mm.	100mm.	4mm.

One plywood seat base   405mm.   340mm.   12mm.

Tools

Jack and smoothing planes, shoulder plane, rule, try square, marking gauge, mortise gauge, marking knife, 8mm. sash mortise chisel, mallet, tenon saw, 25mm. firmer chisel, brace and 12mm. twist bit, wheelbrace and twist drills, hammer, screwdriver, cork rubber and sandpaper, two 1,000mm. sash cramps, four 150mm. 'G' cramps for cramping up former for shaped rail.

Extra Tools required for upholstery

Hacksaw blade, or serrated bread knife, scissors with 9in. blade, tack hammer (upholsterers), sharp knife, pincers.

UPHOLSTERING THE DINING CHAIR

For the base cut a piece of 37mm. thick polyether foam about 6mm. larger than the seat base (see Fig. 60A). A simple method of fixing foam to a seat is shown in Fig. 60B. This is known as a feathered edge, and is made by simply cutting the edges off to make a bevel of approximately 45 degrees.

A strip of calico or self-adhesive tape is stuck on as shown, and the calico or tape is pulled down firmly and is stuck or tacked to the underside.

Covering Material

The material is cut to size and temporarily tacked. It is smoothed over to remove any wrinkles and the tacks are then driven home. The corners are left open to allow for manipulation of corner pleats. This is shown clearly in Fig. 60C, while Fig. 60D shows how the corners are cut to make the pleats. For a neat finish the underside of the seat should be covered with a piece of linette.

Chair Back

Polyether foam 25mm. thick is glued on to the back with a contact adhesive. The cover is cut to size and stitched on the wrong side of the material (see Fig. 60E). The cover after stitching is turned right side out and pulled over the back rail and tacked as shown in the detail.

Note: polyether foam can be cut with a hacksaw blade, serrated bread knife, or scissors with a blade about 9in. long. Wetting the cutting tools when in use will give better results.

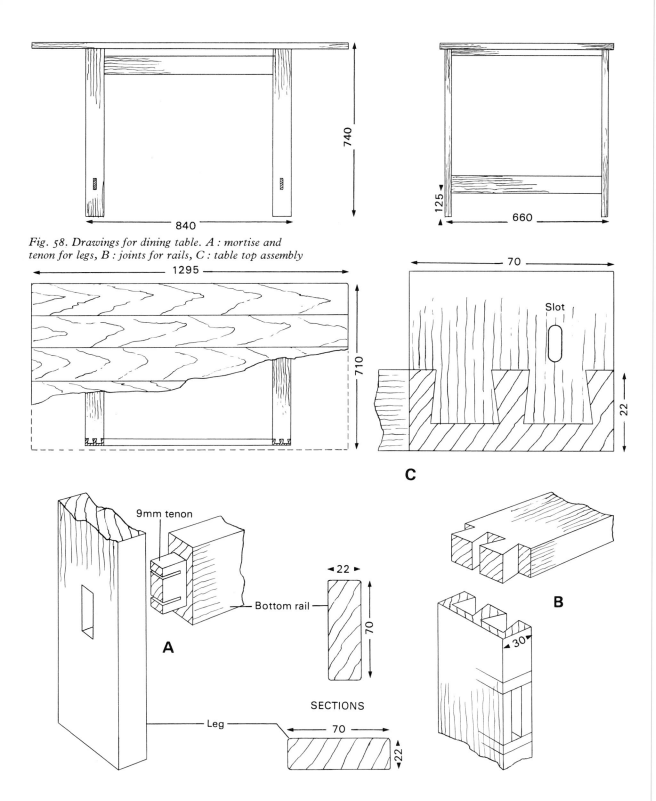

740

840

125

660

Fig. 58. Drawings for dining table. A : mortise and tenon for legs, B : joints for rails, C : table top assembly

1295

710

70

Slot

22

C

9mm tenon

Bottom rail

◄ 22 ►

70

A

SECTIONS

Leg

70

22 ►

◄ 30 ►

B

Plate 14. Tea trolley (page 70)

Material for Upholstery

Polyether or Latex foam, contact adhesive, French chalk or talcum powder for drying off, covering material, linette for underside, 9mm. cut tacks, gimp pins.

15. COFFEE TABLE

This is a small table of pleasing proportions (see Plate 9). It emphasises restraint in the use of material and simplicity in design. The choice of colour for the Formica top should be carefully considered in relation to the wood used, so as to produce a satisfactory colour harmony.

Procedure

1. Prepare all material.
2. Mark out the legs in pairs. The enlarged details (Fig. 61A) show tenon proportions, shaping of legs and top rails.
3. Mark out in pairs the long and short rails; the shoulders are not square on the long rails. Set mortise gauge to a 6mm. mortise chisel and gauge mortises and tenons for side frames.
4. Adjust mortise gauge and mark out mortises on legs for end rails. Make a further adjustment and gauge tenons on end rails.
5. Cut all mortises and tenons, and plough the long rails to take the top before removing tenon cheeks.
6. Fit side frames and test for wind.
7. Taper the inside of the legs, stopping at quadrant as indicated by dotted lines (see Fig. 61A).
8. Make taper on the inside of the leg below end rails.
9. Work shaped bevel on the bottom edge of the side rails, and bevels on the inside top edge. Clean up all inner edges, mask joints and polish.
10. Glue up the side frames, and test the legs for wind. Flush off when glue is set. Polish the inside surface.
11. Shape the end rails and make saw kerfs for wedges. Clean up and polish.

12. Cut the plywood top to size, and plough grooves to receive lipping. The grooves are continued round the top and stop at the leg position. Glue on the Formica.

Adhesive for bonding

The following information on fixing Formica or other types of plastic sheet can be applied to most domestic requirements. The solvent adhesives—of the one-solution impact type, such as Evostik—are simple to use. Adhesion is instantaneous and prolonged pressure is unnecessary. Application: before gluing, lightly sandpaper plastic veneer and plywood base, and clean the surface free from dust, apply the adhesive according to manufacturer's instructions, locate carefully and apply even pressure.

13. Lay the side frames on a cutting board and, using a 6mm. scribing gouge, pare out the 6mm. radius between leg and rail. Clean up with sandpaper and polish.

14. Try table together and make any necessary

Plate 15. Television and drinks cabinet (page 72)

adjustments. Remove horns round the top corners and continue bevel along the top edge. Clean up and polish.

15. Glue up table, carefully driving in wedges. Leave top cramped up until dry.

16. Fit lipping, mitre and glue up. Clean up and complete polishing.

Materials Required

Guarea, utile or sweet chestnut.

CUTTING LIST

Description	Length	Width	Thickness
Four legs	420mm.	40mm.	20mm.
Two side rails	450mm.	40mm.	20mm.
Two end rails	330mm.	25mm.	16mm.
One top, multi-ply	640mm.	320mm.	9mm.
One piece Formica	640mm.	320mm.	1·6mm.
To end lippings	330mm.	22mm.	16mm.
One to cut four side lippings	400mm.	16mm.	12mm.
Oddments for rosewood wedges.			

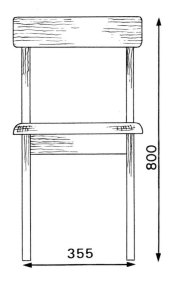

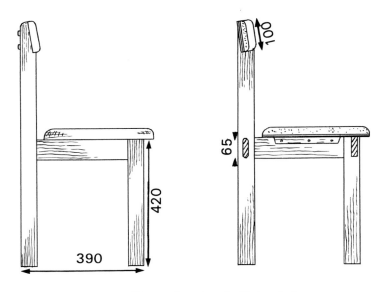

Fig. 59. Drawings for dining chair

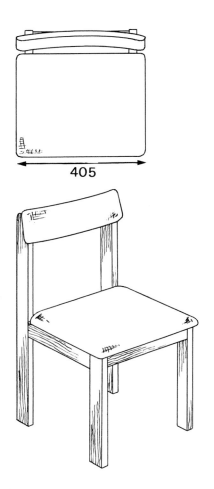

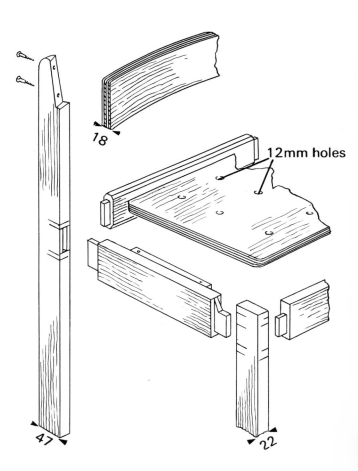

12mm holes

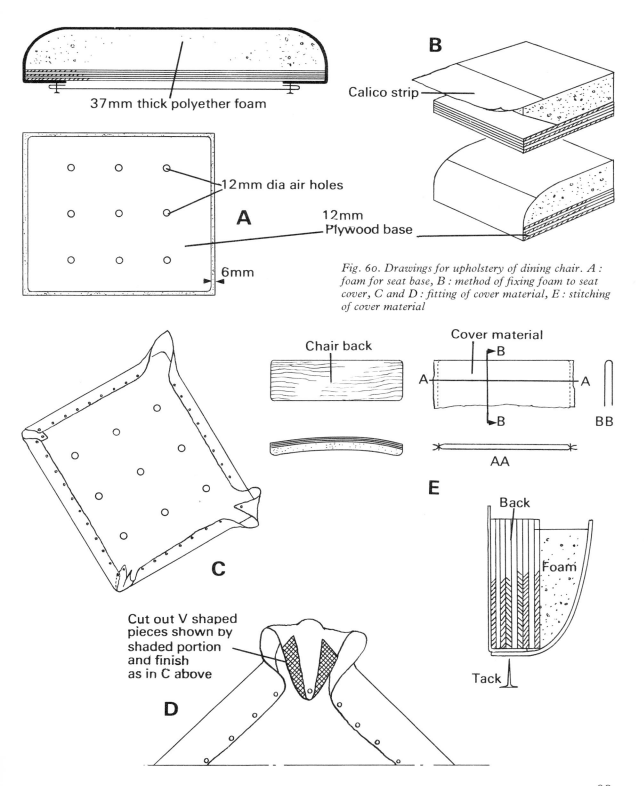

37mm thick polyether foam

12mm dia air holes

A

12mm
Plywood base

6mm

B

Calico strip

Fig. 60. Drawings for upholstery of dining chair. A : foam for seat base, B : method of fixing foam to seat cover, C and D : fitting of cover material, E : stitching of cover material

Chair back

Cover material

B

A — A

B

BB

AA

E

C

Cut out V shaped
pieces shown by
shaded portion
and finish
as in C above

D

Back

Foam

Tack

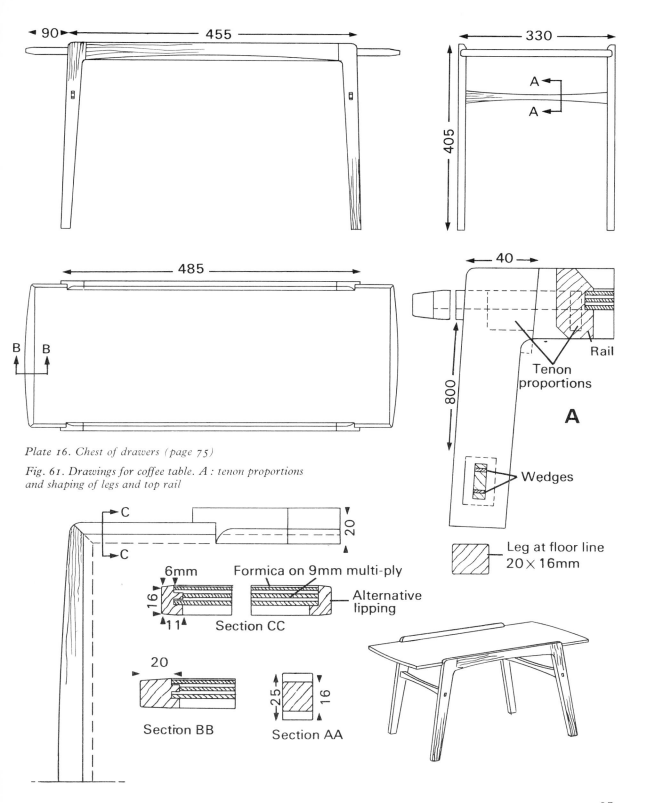

◄ 90 ► ◄——— 455 ———► ◄——— 330 ———►

405

A ◄
A ◄

485

B | B

◄— 40 —►

Rail

Tenon
proportions

800

A

Plate 16. Chest of drawers (page 75)

Fig. 61. Drawings for coffee table. A : tenon proportions
and shaping of legs and top rail

Wedges

Leg at floor line
20 × 16mm

►C

20

►C

6mm   Formica on 9mm multi-ply

16

Alternative
lipping

11   Section CC

20

25   16

Section BB   Section AA

Tools

Jack and smoothing planes, shoulder plane, plough, flat-bottom spokeshave, winding strips, rule, try square, marking gauge, mortise gauge, marking knife, 6mm. sash mortise chisel, mallet, tenon saw, 6mm. scribing gouge, 3mm. and 25mm. firmer chisels, cabinet scraper, cork rubber and sandpaper, hammer, two 760mm. sash cramps.

16. SETTEE

This rather delightful settee in Columbian pine (see Plates 12 and 13), is one of two which were specially designed for the lounge of a small cottage. The main design considerations were: (a) comfort, (b) lightness combined with strength, (c) ease of construction, (d) compact and pleasing appearance, (e) minimum cost.

The top rails of the end frames are finger-jointed, while the bottom rail is stub-tenoned to the legs. All other joints are dowelled.

The 100mm. thick polyether foam seat cushion is supported on 50mm. wide Pirelli webbing.

Fig. 62. Settee showing components and construction

The 75mm. thick foam back cushion is supported by the frame back. Pirelli webbing is stretched and fixed to the stiffening pieces attached to the front and back rails. A shaped compression rail is fixed under these stiffening pieces.

The settee is polished to match the table and chairs already described.

Procedure

1. Prepare all material.
2. Mark out the side frames in pairs.
3. Cut the finger joints and make mortise and tenon joints for bottom rails.
4. Assemble the frames and adjust as necessary.
5. Clean up all the inner surfaces and polish.
6. Glue up the end frames and leave to dry.
7. Mark out the back framing. Cut all vertical rails to length and clean up ends to cut lines.
8. Lay out the pieces forming back framing, number all the joints and mark out dowel locations.
9. Bore holes for dowels. Cut dowels to length (3in. is recommended), fit hand tight. Assemble framing up dry.
10. Make chamfers and clean up all inside surfaces and polish.

Fig. 63. Drawings for settee. A : slots for Pirelli webbing,
B : dowel locations on end frames, C : fitting of webbing

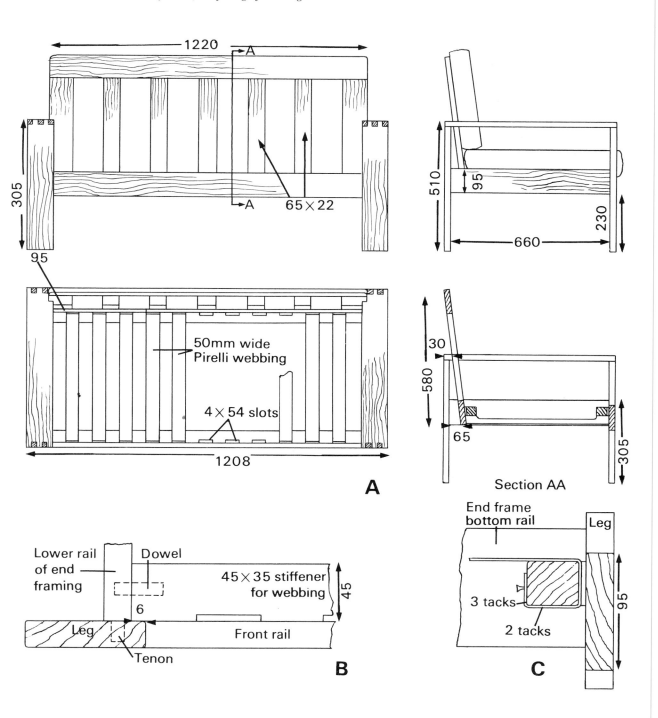

1220

A

A

305

65×22

95

50mm wide
Pirelli webbing

4×54 slots

1208

A

510

95

660

230

30

580

65

305

Section AA

Lower rail
of end
framing

Dowel

45×35 stiffener
for webbing

45

6

Leg

Tenon

Front rail

B

End frame
bottom rail

Leg

3 tacks

2 tacks

95

C

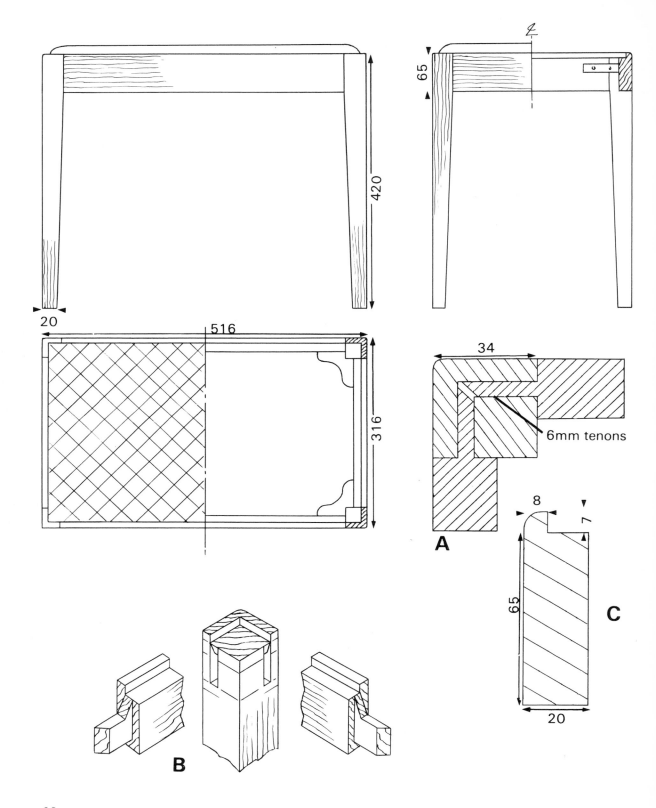

420

20

65

516

316

34

6mm tenons

A

8

7

65

20

C

B

11. Glue up back frame. When dry, flush all joints, clean up and polish.

12. Cut the front rail and the stiffening rails to length. Mark out dowel locations on end frames (see Fig. 63B).

13. Bore holes for dowels. Fit the dowels and assemble back framing and front rail and try up dry.

14. Locate the position for stiffening rails, mark out the make slots for the Pirelli webbing (Fig. 63A).

15. Screw and glue stiffening pieces to front rail and back framing.

16. Prepare cramps and cramping pieces and glue up. Test for squareness and leave to dry.

17. Flush all joints and complete the polishing.

18. Screw the compression rail to stiffeners and fix the Pirelli webbing (Fig. 63C).

19. Make the covers for the cushions.

Materials Required

Columbian pine, sweet chestnut, or oak.

CUTTING LIST

Description	Length	Width	Thickness
Four legs	530mm.	95mm.	22mm.
Four rails	670mm.	95mm.	22mm.
Two back rails	1,230mm.	95mm.	22mm.
One front rail	1,230mm.	95mm.	22mm.
Two vertical end rails	410mm.	95mm.	22mm.
Five vertical rails	410mm.	65mm.	22mm.
Two stiffeners	1,230mm.	45mm.	35mm.
One compression rail (beech)	670mm.	55mm.	25mm.

Three lengths dowel rod 9mm. × 1,220mm.
Eight 55mm. × No. 10 countersunk screws.
Eight metres of 50mm. Pirelli webbing
One seat cushion,
Polyether foam 1,220mm.   610mm.   100mm.
One back cushion,
Polyether foam 1,220mm.   450mm.   75mm.

Tools

Jack and smoothing planes, shoulder plane, flat-bottom spokeshave, winding strips, rule, try square, marking gauge, mortise gauge, marking knife, 9mm. sash mortise chisel, mallet, coping saw, 25mm., 12mm. and 9mm. firmer chisels, brace and dowel bit, wheelbrace and twist drills,

cabinet scraper, cork rubber and sandpaper, screwdriver, hammer, shooting board, four 1,000mm. sash cramps.

17. DRESSING STOOL

This elegant dressing stool (Plate 7) is made in utile. The top is upholstered with polyether foam and covered with furnishing fabric. Many combinations of carcase and upholstery material to suit various colour schemes are possible. The rails of the stool shown in the photograph are decorated with cavetto mouldings. These mouldings can be worked by hand with either a moulding plane or a scratch stock. It is advisable, however, for the inexperienced to make the alternative simple moulding as shown in Fig. 64C. Corner brackets give considerable strength and rigidity to chairs and stools. They are simple to make and fix.

Procedure

1. Prepare the material.

2. Mark out the legs in pairs (see Fig. 64A and B showing the corner joint).

3. Mark out the long and short rails in pairs.

4. Set the mortise gauge to a 6mm. mortise chisel and gauge all mortises and tenons.

5. Chop the mortises and make haunchings on legs.

6. Saw down the tenons. Before cutting the shoulders, work rebate and mouldings on rails.

7. Saw down the shoulders to remove the tenon cheeks, cut the tenons to size and make the haunchings.

8. Mark length of the tenon and mitre the ends (Fig. 64A).

9. Fit all joints. Mark out for rebate on top of legs, and carefully remove waste.

10. Cut legs to length, mark out and taper legs on the inside.

11. Clean up all inside surfaces, mask joints and polish.

12. Glue up the two frames, test the legs for alignment and leave to dry.

13. Flush the joints and clean up.

14. Glue up the end rails and test stool for squareness; leave to dry.

15. Flush all the joints, and complete the mouldings at top of the legs. Clean up and finish polishing.

16. Shape corner brackets, glue and screw in.

17. Cut the plywood base to size and try in rebate. Leave a gap all round to allow for the

Fig. 64. Drawings for upholstered dressing stool. The details shown at A, B and C are referred to in the text

thickness of the covering materials.

18. Bore approximately six 12mm. diameter holes for ventilation in the plywood base.

19. For upholstering, proceed in the same manner as for the dining chair (page 58).

Materials Required
Utile, teak or beech.

CUTTING LIST

Description	Length	Width	Thickness
Four legs	440mm.	34mm.	34mm.
Two side rails	510mm.	65mm.	20mm.
Two end rails	310mm.	65mm.	20mm.
One piece of plywood for base	500mm.	300mm.	9mm.
One piece to make four corner brackets	320mm.	60mm.	22mm.

Tools

Jack and smoothing planes, winding strips, shoulder plane, rebate plane, try square, marking gauge, mortise gauge, 6mm. sash mortise chisel, mallet, tenon saw, bow or pad saw, flat-bottom spokeshave, wood rasp, 25mm. firmer chisel, brace and 12mm. twist bit, wheelbrace and twist drills, cabinet scraper, cork rubber and sandpaper, screwdriver, two 760mm. sash cramps.

18. TEA TROLLEY

A tea trolley is one of the most useful pieces of furniture in the modern home.

The main design features of this trolley are: (a) its small compact dimensions, (b) decorative plastic-surfaced shelves with open ends for easy cleaning, (c) its straightforward constructional features. This design makes a rather nice matching piece to the coffee table illustrated in Plate 9.

The trolley shown in Plate 14 has a slightly modified line, with splayed legs. The main constructional features are similar, but the splayed legs and shoulders are rather more complex than those illustrated in Fig. 65.

Procedure

1. Prepare material.
2. Mark out the legs in pairs.
3. Mark in pairs the top and bottom side rails.
4. Mark out in pairs the top and bottom end rails.

Fig. 65. Drawings for trolley. The details shown at A and B are referred to in the text

Gauge all mortises and tenons. Adjust the gauge as necessary for the end rails.

5. Cut all mortises and tenons. Before cutting the shoulders, make plough grooves in side rails.
6. Finish the shoulders to cut line with shoulder plane.
7. Fit the side frames together and test for wind.
8. Work bevels on side rails as indicated in Fig. 65A. Taper the legs below the bottom rail.
9. Clean up all inner surfaces, mask joints and polish.
10. Glue up the side frames, test for squareness and leave to dry.
11. Flush all joints on the side frames, mark out and continue grooves across legs.
12. Try up the carcase complete with end rails. Mark out and cut the trays to size and apply Formica.
13. Fit in the shelves. The shelves should be fitted hand tight and not forced in with a mallet.
14. Assemble the trolley, cramp up dry and test. Make any necessary adjustments.
15. Polish the end rails. Glue up the trolley and carefully remove surplus glue. Screw through the bottom of the end rails to secure the shelves.
16. Plough lipping and fit to the tray ends (Fig. 65B). Glue up.
17. Clean up and complete polishing.
18. Bore holes to take the wheel fittings.

Materials Required
Guarea, utile or sweet chestnut.

CUTTING LIST

Description	Length	Width	Thickness
Four legs	580mm.	38mm.	22mm.
Four side rails	460mm.	38mm.	22mm.
Four end rails	400mm.	30mm.	22mm.
One top shelf, in multi-ply	600mm.	400mm.	12mm.
One bottom shelf, in multi-ply	600mm.	400mm.	12mm.
Two pieces of Formica	600mm.	400mm.	1.6mm.
Four pieces for lipping	550mm.	22mm.	12mm.

Four rubber-tyred casters, 65mm. diameter.
Eight 38mm. × No. 8 countersunk brass screws for fixing shelves to end rails.

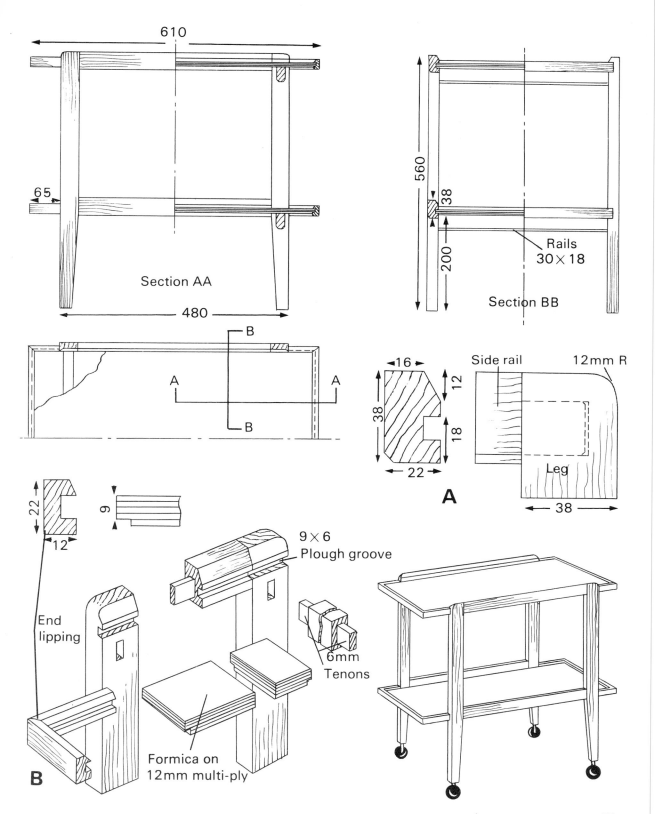

610

65

480

Section AA

B

A   A

B

560

38

200

Rails
30 × 18

Section BB

16

12

38

18

22

Side rail

12mm R

Leg

38

A

22

12

9

End
lipping

9 × 6
Plough groove

6mm
Tenons

Formica on
12mm multi-ply

B

Tools

Jack and smoothing planes, plough plane, shoulder plane, rebate plane, winding strips, rule, try square, marking gauge, mortise gauge, marking knife, 6mm. sash mortise chisel, mallet, tenon saw, 9mm. and 25mm. firmer chisels, brace and 9mm. twist bit, wheelbrace and twist drills, cabinet scraper, cork rubber and sandpaper, screwdriver, hammer, two 760mm. sash cramps.

19. TELEVISION STAND AND DRINKS CABINET

This job was specifically designed to serve in the dual capacity of a television stand and a drinks cabinet. Plate 15 shows the cabinet with doors closed. It is well proportioned and of a convenient height for television viewing. The provision of castors gives the cabinet the added advantage of mobility and ease of adjustment when viewing.

The carcase is in parana pine, and has two teak doors, with bead and butt panels. The interior is fitted with a shaped shelf which caters for the storage of a good range of glasses as well as providing adequate space for tall-necked bottles. The carcase is made with bare-faced housing joints (Fig. 66A), which are reinforced with 8mm. teak dowels. An alternative design (shown in Fig. 67A) has flush doors and small turned handles. Figs. 66, 67 and 68 show the constructional details of the cabinet.

Procedure

1. Prepare all material for carcase and shelf.
2. To obtain the width, each end is made up of two boards and edge-jointed. With a trying plane 'shoot the edges' of the boards—'shoot' is the technical term for planing an edge straight—and glue up. This joint can be reinforced with dowels, in which case it is known as a dowelled edge joint.
3. Shoot the boards to make the top and bottom of the cabinet, and glue up.
4. Clean up the sides, top and bottom, and prepare for marking out.
5. Mark out in pairs and shape the ends.
6. Cut the housings and make rebate for back.
7. Mark out the top and bottom, cut to size, and make tongues.
8. Carefully fit the top and bottom and test for

squareness. Make the shelf and fit to the carcase.
9. Make the mouldings on top and bottom of ends and assemble the carcase dry.
10. Clean up all inner surfaces and polish.
11. Prepare teak dowels.
12. Prepare the sash cramps and cramping blocks and glue up the carcase. Test for squareness and leave to dry.
13. Mark out the dowel positions, bore holes and glue in the dowels. Flush off when dry.
14. Fit the back and screw in. Fit and scribe the back rail over the ends (see Fig. 66A) and glue in.
15. Prepare all material for the doors.
16. Mark out the stiles in pairs, and number all the joints for easy identification.
17. Mark out the rails in pairs. (Fig. 67 shows the rails paired up and the method of setting out). Meeting stiles: these are also shown on Fig. 67. Note the relationship of the centre line and bead. The small rosewood handle is dovetailed into the edge of the bead.
18. Chop all the mortises and cut tenons before making plough grooves.
19. Fig. 67 shows the stiles and rails partly ploughed. The ploughing must be completed before the shoulders are cut.
20. Fit the joints and assemble the doors up dry.
21. Cut the panels to size and make the tongues all round. Make the bead on the edges of the panels.
22. Fit the panels, clean up the beads and all inner surfaces, glue up.
23. Flush all the joints and clean up doors. Finish with linseed oil (see under Wood Finishing in Chapter Three).
24. Fit doors to the carcase and prepare for hinging.
25. Set marking gauges to suit the butts, let the hinges into the edges of the doors (Fig. 68). (See also Chapter Four for information on hinging).
26. Offer up the door to the carcase and mark hinge location as shown in Fig. 68.
27. Remove the waste on the carcase side and fit the hinges.
28. Hang the doors and adjust as necessary. Fit the handle and ball catches.
29. Fit the teak moulding to the edge of the interior shelf (Fig. 66B).
30. Attach the castors, and complete polishing.

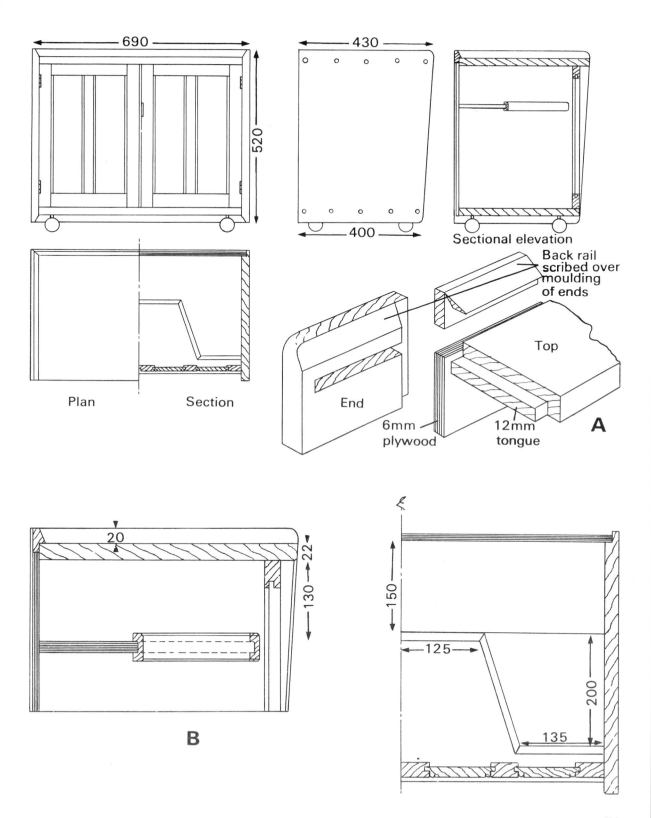

690

520

430

400

Sectional elevation

Plan

Section

Back rail
scribed over
moulding
of ends

End

Top

6mm
plywood

12mm
tongue

A

20

22

130

B

150

125

200

135

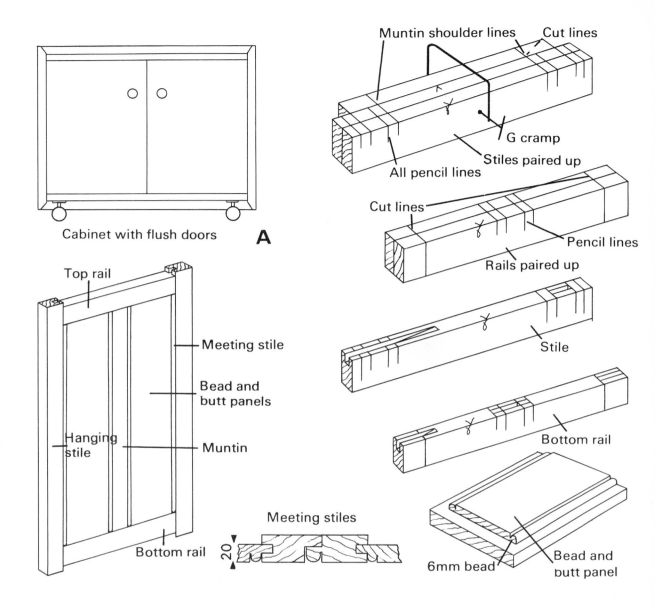

Cabinet with flush doors **A**

Top rail

Meeting stile

Bead and butt panels

Hanging stile

Muntin

Bottom rail

Meeting stiles

20

Muntin shoulder lines   Cut lines

G cramp

All pencil lines   Stiles paired up

Cut lines

Pencil lines

Rails paired up

Stile

Bottom rail

6mm bead   Bead and butt panel

Materials Required

Parana pine, for carcase.
Teak, for the panelled doors, or Columbian pine and teak.

Fig. 67. Details for television and drinks cabinet. A: the alternative flush doors

CUTTING LIST

Description	Length	Width	Thickness
Four pieces, to make two ends	580mm.	225mm.	22mm.
Two pieces for top	690mm.	225mm.	22mm.
Two pieces for bottom	690mm.	205mm.	22mm.
Back rail	690mm.	30mm.	22mm.
Back, plywood	690mm.	520mm.	6mm.
One piece for shelf, plywood	680mm.	155mm.	12mm.

Two pieces for
    shelf, plywood 215mm.   196mm.   12mm.
One piece of
    lipping to
    cut five   950mm.   25mm.   12mm.
Twenty dowels   60mm.   8mm. dia.

Doors with bead and butt panels:
Two hinging
    stiles   515mm.   38mm.   20mm.
Two meeting
    stiles   515mm.   44mm.   20mm.
Two bottom
    rails   325mm.   45mm.   20mm.
Two top rails   325mm.   38mm.   20mm.
Two muntins   460mm.   30mm.   20mm.
Four panels   410mm.   120mm.   15mm.
Twenty 16mm. × No. 6 brass screws for back.
Four 50mm. diameter castors.
Two pairs of 50mm. solid drawn brass butts and
screws.
Two adjustable ball catches.

Tools

Jack, trying and smoothing planes, shoulder
plane, rebate and plough planes, flat-bottom
spokeshave, panel and tenon saws, winding
strips, rule, try square, marking gauges, mortise
gauge, marking knife, 6mm. sash mortise chisel,
mallet, 12mm. and 25mm. firmer chisels, brace
and bits, wheelbrace and twist drills, cabinet
scraper, cork rubber and sandpaper, screwdriver, hammer, four 1,000mm. sash cramps.

20. CHEST OF DRAWERS

The pleasing and colourful four-drawer chest
shown in Plate 16 provides ample storage facili-
ties and makes a most useful piece of furniture
for the bedroom. The making of the chest should
present little difficulty to the man who has
worked successfully through Chapter Five making joints and simple practice jobs. The chest is
made in deal with a framing module of 45mm. ×
20mm. and can be painted to harmonise with any
colour scheme.

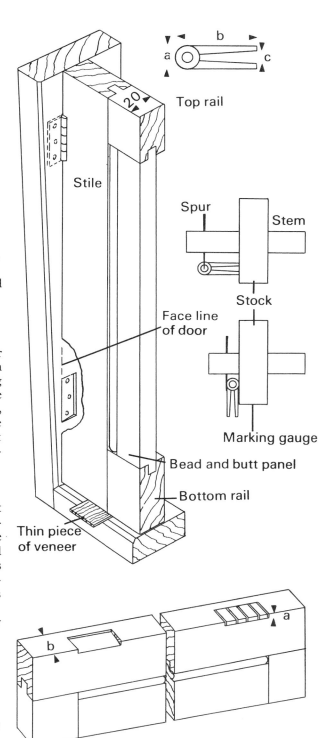

*Fig. 68. Details for television and drinks cabinet, showing
the marking out of positions of butts on carcase ends and
the method of hinging*

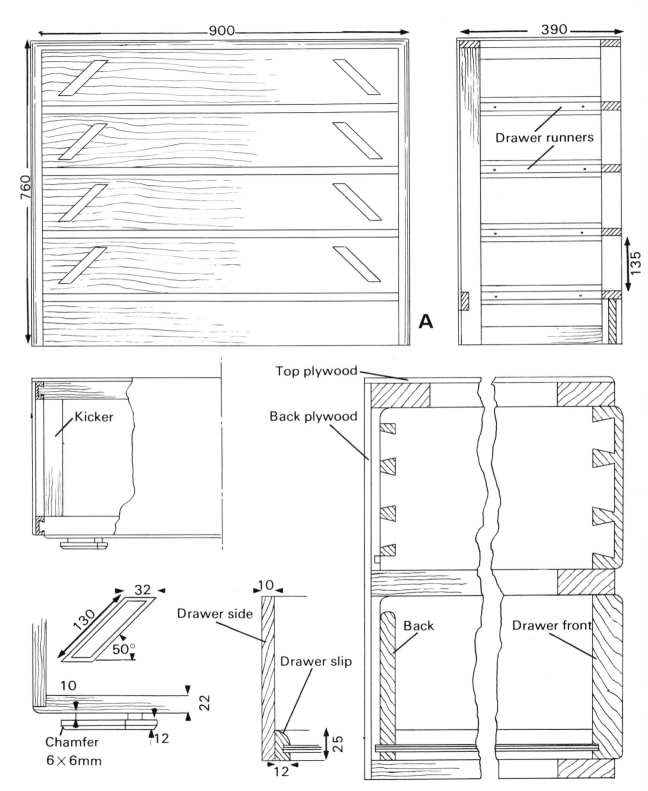

900

760

390

Drawer runners

135

A

Kicker

Top plywood

Back plywood

32

130

50°

10

Drawer side

Drawer slip

Back

Drawer front

10

22

Chamfer
6×6mm

12

12

25

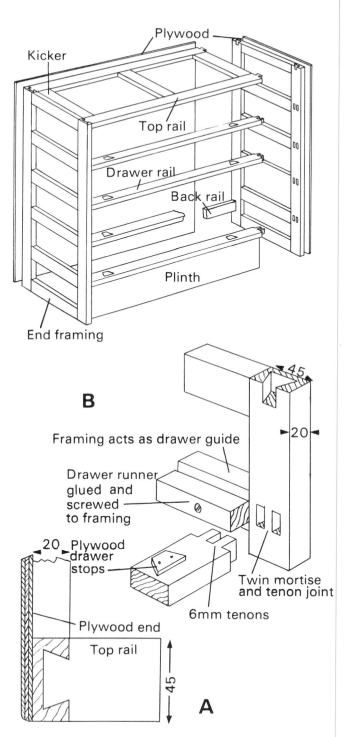

The main constructional features are: (a) mortise and tenon or dowelled joints for the end frames, (b) top rails dovetailed to end frames, (c) twin mortise and tenon joints at drawer rails preventing the drawer rails from twisting, (d) end and top frames faced with 4mm. plywood. The back, which is also of 4mm. plywood, is simply pinned on. Each drawer handle is made up of two pieces of beech, which are glued together and finally secured to the drawer fronts. Figs. 69, 70 and 71 show the details of construction.

Procedure

1. Prepare all material.
2. Mark out the end frames, cut to size and prepare for dowelling.
3. Glue up the end frames, and when dry, flush all joints.
4. Cut plywood panels to fit end frames. Glue and cramp panels to framing. When dry, carefully flush plywood edges. Round the front edges as shown in Fig. 70A.
5. Cut the top rails to length. Mark out and cut dovetails and fit to the end frames.
6. Mark out the four drawer rails and cut twin tenons. Make mortises on end frames to suit.
7. Cut drawer kickers and centre top rail to size, and tenon to framing.
8. Mark out the lower back rail and tenon into end frames.
9. Assemble the carcase dry and adjust as necessary.
10. Prepare for gluing up, have all cramps and cramping blocks ready.
11. Glue up carcase, test for square and leave to dry.
12. Fit plinth and secure with blocks glued to end framing and bottom drawer rail.
13. Fit drawer runners. Glue and screw to end framing (Fig. 70B). Note: these must be lined up carefully with drawer rails.
14. Cut and fit drawer fronts to carcase. Note: to allow for fitting, the drawer fronts at this stage should be tight and only enter the carcase approx. 2mm. (see Fig. 71B).

Fig. 70. *Exploded view of chest of drawers showing construction. A : top rails dovetailed to ends, B : fitting of drawer runners and twin mortise and tenon joints*

15. Cut drawer backs to size.

16. Cut drawer sides to length, and mark out for lap dovetails at drawer front, and through dovetails and drawer back. Note: an alternative drawer construction, using simple lap and housing joints, is shown in Fig. 71C.

17. Check thickness of plywood bottoms and make plough grooves in drawer fronts to suit.

18. Prepare drawer slips and muntins and make plough grooves to take plywood bottoms. Note: for drawers over 600mm. in length it is necessary to fit muntins to reinforce the bottom. See drawer construction, Fig. 71A.

19. Assemble drawers and glue up. Test diagonally for squareness, and leave to dry.

20. Glue in drawer slips and muntins. (The muntins are tongued into the drawer fronts and housed into the drawer backs).

21. Fit drawers to slide freely and fix drawer stops with glue and pins. Note: to assist free running of drawers, rub a little candle grease on bottom edges.

22. Make handles and screw to drawer fronts.

23. Cut top to size and glue to framing. Clean up and round edges.

24. Cut the back to size and panel pin to framing.

25. Clean up carcase and drawer fronts, remove handles and prepare for painting.

CUTTING LIST

Description	Length	Width	Thickness
Four stiles	765mm.	45mm.	20mm.
Twelve rails	330mm.	45mm.	20mm.
Two top rails	900mm.	45mm.	20mm.
Four drawer rails	900mm.	45mm.	20mm.
Two kickers	320mm.	45mm.	20mm.
One centre support	320mm.	45mm.	20mm.
One back rail	900mm.	45mm.	20mm.
One plinth	900mm.	135mm.	20mm.
Eight drawer runners	320mm.	20mm.	20mm.
Two pieces for ends, plywood	760mm.	390mm.	4mm.
One top, plywood	900mm.	390mm.	4mm.

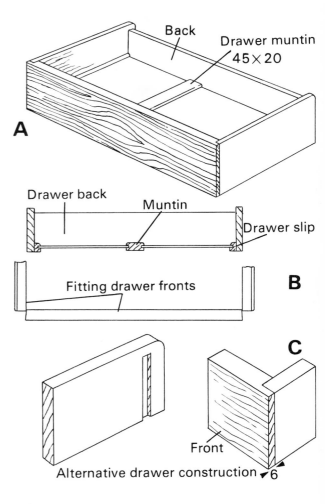

Fig. 71. Construction of drawers. A: pictorial view, B: fitting of drawer fronts to carcase, C: alternative drawer construction

One back,			
plywood	900mm.	700mm.	4mm.
Four drawer			
fronts	900mm.	140mm.	22mm.
Eight drawer			
slides	380mm.	140mm.	10mm.
Four drawer			
backs	900mm.	120mm.	10mm.
Four muntins	380mm.	45mm.	20mm.
Eight drawer			
slips	380mm.	25mm.	12mm.
One to cut eight			
drawer bottoms,			
plywood	400mm.	25mm.	6mm.
Eight pieces for			
drawer bottoms,			
plywood	425mm.	380mm.	4mm.
Drawer handles in beech:			
One piece to			
cut eight	1,200mm.	32mm.	12mm.

One piece to cut eight 1,120mm. 22mm. 10mm.
Sixteen 38mm. No. 8 countersunk iron screws for handles
Thirty 18mm. panel pins for back
Sixteen 12mm. panel pins for drawer stops
Sixteen 32mm. No. 8 countersunk iron screws for drawer runners.

Tools

Jack and smoothing planes; plough and rebate planes; rule; try square; marking gauge; mortise gauge; 6mm. sash mortise chisel; mallet; hammer, dovetail template; tenon, dovetail and panel saws; 25mm., 18mm. and 6mm. firmer chisels; brace and 6mm. dowel bit; wheelbrace and twist drills; two 600mm. sash cramps; two 1,150mm. sash cramps; screwdriver; cork rubber; sandpaper.

Acknowledgements

Assistance given by the following in the preparation of this book is gratefully acknowledged by the author and publishers.
Stanley Works (G.B.) Ltd., for Figs. 6, 7, 10 and 18.
C. and J. Hampton Ltd., for Figs. 5, 8, 12, 14 and 16.
William Ridgway and Sons Ltd., for Fig. 25.

Messrs. Habitat, for the following accessories: the egg cup and saucer in Plate 4, the white vase in Plate 5, the fabric in Plate 8, and the table lamp in Plate 16.
Goods and Chattels Ltd., for the following accessories: the saucepan in Plate 1 and the candlestick holder in Plate 7.
Laurence Gall, who took the photographs for Figs. 22, 23, 30, 32, 45 and 62.

972